Student Handbook to Sociology

Social Structure
Organizations and Institutions

Volume III

Student Handbook to Sociology

Social Structure
Organizations and Institutions

Volume III

ROBERT M. ORRANGE

Liz Grauerholz
General Editor

Facts On File

An Infobase Learning Company

Student Handbook to Sociology: Social Structure
Copyright © 2012 Robert M. Orrange

Facts On File, Inc.
An Imprint of Infobase Learning
132 West 31st Street
New York NY 10001

Library of Congress Cataloging-in-Publication Data
Student handbook to sociology / Liz Grauerholz, general editor.
   v. cm.
  Includes bibliographical references and index.
   Contents: v. 1. Histories and theories — v. 2. Research methods — v. 3. Social structure — v. 4. Socialization — v. 5. Stratification and inequality — v. 6. Deviance and crime — v. 7. Social change.
   ISBN 978-0-8160-8314-5 (alk. paper) — ISBN 978-0-8160-8315-2 (v. 1 : alk. paper) — ISBN 978-0-8160-8316-9 (v. 2 : alk. paper) — ISBN 978-0-8160-8317-6 (v. 3 : alk. paper) — ISBN 978-0-8160-8319-0 (v. 4 : alk. paper) — ISBN 978-0-8160-8320-6 (v. 5 : alk. paper) — ISBN 978-0-8160-8321-3 (v. 6 : alk. paper) — ISBN 978-0-8160-8322-0 (v. 7 : alk. paper)
1. Sociology. I. Grauerholz, Elizabeth, 1958-
   HM585.S796 2012
   301--dc23
                                    2011025983

Facts On File books are available at special discounts when purchased in bulk quantities for businesses, associations, institutions, or sales promotions. Please call our Special Sales Department at (212) 967-8800 or (800) 322-8755.

You can find Facts On File on the World Wide Web at
http://www.infobaselearning.com

Text design and composition by Erika K. Arroyo
Cover printed by Yurchak Printing, Landisville, Pa.
Book printed and bound by Yurchak Printing, Landisville, Pa.
Date Printed: April 2012
Printed in the United States of America

10 9 8 7 6 5 4 3 2 1

CONTENTS

FOREWORD

One of the gifts that sociology offers is insight into making what is invisible within our social world "visible." Nowhere is this more important or true than in the realm of social structure and social institutions. The fact is, we live every moment of our lives within social institutions, yet most of us are oblivious to this "structure" and how our lives are patterned and shaped by larger forces. Yet, there is no aspect of our lives—including that which we consider most private and personal—that is not shaped by social structure. Even when you feel most spontaneous and in touch with your "true self," you do so within a social framework that gives rise to these types of experiences, validates some experiences (and not others), and most of all, guides their expression.

In this volume, Robert Orrange makes visible the ways in which our lives are shaped by social structure. He examines the many ways in which stable and recurring patterns of behavior characterize society and social relationships. The major ways we experience social structure is through involvement with social institutions, and this concept is the primary focus of this volume. You will learn about the most influential institutions, including the family, politics, economy, education, religion, and media. You will also learn how these institutions shape our world, give meaning to our daily lives, and allow for communities to build important and sustaining ties.

As this volume shows, social institutions are not static or unchanging. Indeed, each emerged due to particular social needs and dynamics, and each change as these social forces shift. Only by understanding these dynamics and social forces can we make informed decisions about what type of change is most beneficial—not to a few individuals, as sometimes happens—but to society as a whole. Thus, this volume serves not only as the basis for understanding the many other issues that concern sociologists and are explored in future volumes, but also as a vehicle that will help you acquire the insight necessary to meeting the challenges facing our ever-changing social world.

—Liz Grauerholz, University of Central Florida

INTRODUCTION

Social structure shapes, directs, and influences virtually every aspect of social life. From a simple handshake to the inauguration of a president, social structure exerts its looming presence in all manner of human affairs, great and small. At a most basic level, it refers to persistent and recurring patterns of human behavior. In this volume, we explore broader, more generalized, and organized manifestations of social structure to assist readers in understanding the basic patterns of activity that govern our world. These general patterns are to be found in what are known as social institutions, or major arenas of social life, which have distinct goals, ends, or purposes, and in which individuals play unique roles. Social institutions do not simply guide and direct our behavior; they also teach us as to what it means to be human. They shape our self-understandings, ends, and purposes, even as we navigate through these to achieve those very ends and purposes.

The core social institutions having greatest impact upon our lives include the economy, a domain in which valued resources are generated, transformed, and distributed throughout society. In the case of U.S. society, the economic process is carried out primarily by buyers and sellers in a marketplace. Related to the economy is the institution of politics and government, which reflects our need to establish collective goals and priorities as a society, and then to mobilize the resources needed to achieve those ends. For us, this involves the practice of representative democracy, where we elect fellow citizens to independent ruling bodies to carry out the collective will of the people. Another major social institution is found in the more intimate realm of family (and sometimes friendship) and involves cooperation, nurturing, and care among its members, with a special emphasis on meeting the needs of dependents. We also have the social institution of religion, which involves beliefs and practices focused on notions

1

of the sacred or the divine. Then, there is the institution of education, the means by which society transmits knowledge to its members. And finally, there is the mass media, another system by which information and knowledge, but also advertising and entertainment, are transmitted to and throughout society.

In exploring the nature of social structure through an understanding of social institutions, we place special emphasis upon how social institutions in the modern world tend to be structured in a powerful and unique way, specifically through formal organizations, or bureaucracies. Most of our institutions are manifest, or put into practice, through complex organizations—large impersonal groups organized around a specific goal or purpose. This view of our modern industrial world is fundamental, yet rarely appreciated. In the end, however, it is these two key characteristics of social structure—social institutions and their modern manifestation in formal, typically bureaucratic, organizations—that are essential for understanding how our lives are structured, the freedoms we enjoy, and the constraints we face as members of contemporary society.

CHAPTER 1

WHAT IS SOCIAL STRUCTURE? THE ROLE OF ORGANIZATIONS AND INSTITUTIONS

Social structure refers to stable and recurring patterns of behavior, which invariably involve relationships with other people. Such simple gestures as a waved "hello," a hand shake, or even a simple, "Hey" reflect patterned behaviors that enable us to carry out our activities with some degree of security and predictability. Just think how offended, anxious, or confused we feel when we make such gestures and others do not respond to them. As you explore social structure through the pages of this book, you will come to see that it is to be found virtually everywhere and that without the social structural patterns that shape and direct our behavior, life would be virtually impossible.

To illustrate this important point, consider the following vignette:

> Upon entering her first semester at college, Lisa felt a sense of excitement and anticipation but also a great deal of anxiety about what this new experience would bring. In many ways, it was very different from the high school world to which she had grown accustomed. High school was one big building in which all of her classes were located. The school day was more or less fixed, beginning way too early at 7:50 a.m. when the first bell rang for home room. Thereafter, a series of bells rang to signal the orderly movement (with a little predicable chaos thrown in) of students and teachers from one class period and subject matter to another, with breaks for lunch, and perhaps other activities, and with one final bell signaling the end of the formal school day precisely at 2:50 p.m.

College life was different. She had to navigate an entire campus having many different administrative and classroom buildings. And students came and went freely at virtually all hours of the day. She had most of her classes during the day, but returned to campus on Thursday evening for a night class. And she was certainly both excited and anxious about her classes. At first, she was unsure about what to expect from her professors, but after writing a few assignments and taking a couple of exams, she realized that (with the exception of one class) she was starting to get the hang of things. In fact, there was a lot about the academic side of college life that had a familiar ring to it. Oh, it was more demanding, and she felt a great deal of personal responsibility for her own success, but she soon came to see that her high school experience had gone far in preparing her for what was to come at this next phase in life, with the exception of needing a little extra help in her math class. And this she was able to obtain quite easily after her professor recommended a tutor for her. In the end, it looked like she was going to be alright.

This vignette could very well reflect, to a greater or lesser extent, the experience of countless young adults who make the transition from high school to college at the beginning of autumn each year. And, in certain respects, it is likely reflective a larger range of experiences by which all sorts of people make transitions to new phases in their lives, many of which at first bring forth a measure of anticipation, uncertainty, even angst, but eventually lead to new habits and predictable patterns in due time. One of the reasons why we are able to experience a good measure of order and predictability in our everyday lives, even in such a complex world, has to do with what sociologists call social structure. And social structure is what this book is all about.

SOCIAL STRUCTURE

Although sociologists use the term "social structures" to denote social rather than physical realities, these structures can be viewed in much the same way we view physical structures, such as roads, bridges, or buildings. Physical structures, in fact, invariably involve and are characterized by social elements. First and foremost, physical structures guide and shape, or pattern, our behavior. Automobiles are designed to be driven on paved roads (if we keep all terrain vehicles out of the discussion for a moment), and so we must follow those predefined patterns laid out for us by the grid of roads and highways that make up the dominant arteries of transportation in society. It is, nonetheless, kind of amazing that a little painted line in the middle of a highway has the power to keep the two-way opposing flows of traffic separate the vast majority of the time. We all know to stay to the right, unless we're in England or a handful of other countries, where drivers know they are to stay to the left.

Social structure guides and directs our behavior much like the flow of traffic on a highway. *(Shutterstock)*

Social structure is to be found virtually everywhere around us, and without its patterns that shape and direct our behavior, life would be virtually impossible. In the vignette presented earlier in this chapter, Lisa was able to successfully adjust to her new life as a college student. While everything may have seemed to be new and perplexing at first, she soon established a new set of patterns or routines. The important thing to remember here is that she was able to do it largely in part due to her earlier experience in high school. Schools, be they at the primary, secondary, or even tertiary (college) level, all seem to have some generalized patterns or structures in common. Teachers, students, specific times and locations for classes, exams, quizzes, papers, etc., are all recurring features of this realm we call education. The individual pieces and players may be different, but the social structures remain more or less the same.

There are, in fact, many other realms besides education where such predictable patterns and structures can be observed, and we will introduce these later in the chapter and explore them in greater depth throughout the book. However, we must first address the all encompassing character and quality of social structure, which is to be found everywhere and is involved in virtually everything we do. Because it is one of the most all-encompassing concepts in sociology, it is also one of the most difficult concepts to pin down. We can say so much about it that we risk creating so much confusion that the discussion becomes about nothing at all. And so, in order to begin making sense of social structure, we must first briefly introduce another related concept—one that is also vast, all encompassing, and runs the risk of being about everything and nothing at the same time. That concept is **culture**.

CULTURE

Social structure is intimately connected to the idea of culture, a concept with which we are all generally familiar. Sociologists generally define **culture** as the beliefs, values, norms, symbols, language, material objects, and technology that define a people's way of life. It is what we call a "totalizing" concept because it covers just about everything. But as we explore certain (not all) elements of culture, we can begin to select those which are important for making sense of social structure. We'll begin at the beginning of the list included in our definition of culture.

Beliefs are statements that we hold to be true. For instance, we believe in equality. Consistent with this belief, schools today make involvement in a wide range of sports highly accessible for girls. In the not so distant past (just a few decades ago), there were few such options for school girls. In fact, it was believed that sports were really for boys, and that girls generally had neither the interest nor the aptitude for sports.

Values reflect very broad standards or guides for living. They define what is desirable in life, the ends or goals of our behaviors and our striving. In the 1960s, sociologist Robin Williams formulated what he perceived to be the ten key values of American culture. Whenever I teach introductory sociology at the college level, I share these with my students who have consistently confirmed them as being central to how they understand the culture in our contemporary world. A subset of these values includes individual achievement and success, material comforts, along with progress and science. So how do these affect us in patterned (structured) ways? Consider the fact that ever since you have been a student (really most of your life) you have likely been continuously evaluated and graded, something Williams would link to our focus on achievement and success.

You can observe other ways that values such as material comfort, progress and science, shape our lives. We have an economic system where people can try out creative new ideas and then take risks by starting businesses aimed at selling products and services based on these ideas; if successful, they will be able to enjoy the affluence, material rewards, and comforts that accompany their success. Or, consider how our society is constantly embracing progress in the form of new technologies (which are of course dependent upon continuous growth in scientific knowledge) to such an extent that fundamental patterns by which people expect to communicate are rapidly changing. When I was growing up, there were no cell phones or personal computers. Instead we contacted family and friends via the family telephone or sent letters by mail. These were the dominant patterns of communication, but they have been transformed at an ever more rapid pace over recent decades. It's easy to imagine that just in the time you have been reading this chapter you have either sent or received a text message to a family member or friend.

Arguably, the element of culture that is most central and relevant to our understanding of social structure is the idea of norms. **Norms** can be thought of as rules for behavior, the dos and don'ts of everyday life. In fact, they can also be thought of as structures, and they cover a wide range of phenomena. Going back to our discussion of driving, for example, we can see that the norm in the United States is to drive on the right side of the road. And, if we do not follow this norm, others will take notice and are likely to respond to our violation in some way (e.g., honking, waving, shouting, or calling the police). In the examples about college life, we also saw norms, for example, fixed times at which classes begin and end. Coming to class late can be uncomfortable and embarrassing for students; for professors, a student not observing and honoring this norm might be annoying. It is easy to see that such norms have real power to influence behavior.

THE NORMATIVE ORDER

Out of all the complex facets of culture, norms, or the normative order, hold the greatest significance for understanding social structure. As we mentioned, norms guide our behavior in various social situations. They set standards and expectations for how we should behave. We are not born with a sense of what the norms of our culture should be, but instead learn them from others (parents, siblings, teachers, role models, and friends) over time. In the process, we internalize them in such a way that they become part of who we are, and we come to take many of them for granted. And yet, in a complex society such as ours, with so many subgroups based on region, race-ethnicity, religion, and/or social class, we inevitably become reflective about many of the norms we embrace and follow. There is a tendency to question them, adopting some and discarding others. The normative order is not necessarily uniform across all groups and situations, but we can still point to an ongoing normative order.

In thinking about norms as dos and don'ts, rules and guidelines, the question arises as to who will enforce the norms should some choose not to follow them? The short answer to that question is, we all do! We do so in the form of **sanctions**, or penalties exacted for the violation of a norm. For instance, you and a friend are waiting in line at a movie theatre, and someone unwittingly cuts in front of you. Oftentimes a simple clarification ("Excuse me, but we're already in line") calls attention to the individual's behavior, and to the violation of the norm related to waiting in line and is enough to motivate the individual to take his proper place at the end of the line. But norms may not always be as clear cut to all parties involved in social interaction. At times they may be fluid in nature, sometimes emerging in the course of interaction. We can use our example about waiting in line to illustrate this point. Questions may arise among the individuals involved as to the exact nature of the line. Where does it begin and end? Does the norm of forming a line even apply to the particular situation at hand? To the specific individuals involved? In situations where the norm is unclear or questionable, interpersonal conflict may ensue, particularly in cases where someone feels slighted, affronted, or treated with disrespect.

The above example deals with what sociologists refer to as **negative sanctions**. Perhaps a clearer example of a negative sanction would be when a child repeatedly misbehaves at the dinner table and the parent responds by sending the child to his room without dessert. But there are also **positive sanctions**,

The normative order tends keeps everyone in line. If we get out of line, sanctions may force us back in. *(Shutterstock)*

which reward compliance with a given normative order. These occur when people respond to a norm in a manner that reinforces its collective value to the group. Thus, going back to our movie theatre example, two individuals arrive at the ticket window simultaneously. One says to the other, "Oh, I believe you were here first. You go ahead," and gets a smile and a "Thank you very much" as a reward. Along similar lines, if our misbehaving child mends his ways at the dinner table on the following night and politely eats all of his vegetables during the meal, his parents may offer him a special dessert as a reward for his good behavior.

These examples illustrate a type of norm introduced by sociologist William Graham Sumner roughly a century ago in his classic work, *Folkways*. **Folkways** are the everyday practices and customs that guide the ongoing activities of people in any given society. They take on a kind of second nature, or unquestioned common sense, for the entire society. School is a place where many folkways operate and can be easily observed. For example, students know they are supposed to quiet down and listen when a teacher motions that she is about to begin class; they recognize that they are to be sitting at their desks, prepared to take notes. Shortly after a student has been introduced to the educational system, he also learns that violating one of these folkways incurs informal verbal sanctions. Responding quickly to the violation, a teacher will say, "Jimmy, I'll be leading the class discussion from here on out" or "We all know that the windowsill is not a desk."

Sumner also introduced the term **mores** to refer to norms that are of great moral significance to the society. Violating a more is a far greater infraction than violating a norm and invites serious and powerful negative sanctions. In fact, these tend to be so powerful that they are rarely debated—both the actions and the corresponding sanctions are fully understood. In U.S. society, acts such as murder, rape, or incest, elicit deep and powerful reactions from people; they result in serious negative sanctions that are of a vastly greater order of magnitude than sanctions imposed for violation of folkways.

In developing his insights about folkways and mores, Sumner was thinking primarily about preindustrial, tribal communities, in which all members knew one another, and norms were widely shared and collectively understood. But even in our own complex, modern society, it is still very useful to draw upon folkways and mores in thinking about the normative order. Over centuries, many of the more serious yet informal and widely understood normative definitions have been formally codified into law. At the same time, associated informal sanctions have developed into formal social controls. And so, we can think of our legal system as a complex of formalized norms, the violation of which elicits formal social controls. For instance, if someone gets caught robbing a bank or committing a murder, that person will more than likely be detained by the police, tried in a court of law, and if found guilty, formally punished by having to spend many years in a state-sponsored prison. Another way in which norms have become more formalized in our society is through rules and policies that apply in specific domains, such as in schools and in the workplace. For instance, a student who comes to school late is sent to the principal's office for a permission slip, or an employee who arrives late to work may get written up by his supervisor, but in all likelihood, the police will not be called in these instances.

ACTORS AND SOCIAL RELATIONSHIPS

Thus far, we have used examples to show how we rely upon social structure—and more precisely, norms—to navigate daily life. The normative order enables us to feel a sense of order, security, and control, but it also set limits and constraints regarding what is permissible in social situations. But just who are the "we" in this equation? And are norms for any given situation the same for all of us? These are questions that sociologists address in studying group life and society and the individuals who populate the society in question. In sociological parlance, the term **actor** is used to represent the person, the very unique and complex individual who takes part in group life. And, it is this actor who draws upon norms to make sense of social situations and take appropriate action.

In our examples above, we noted how the *teacher* motions to the *students* that class is about to begin; that *students* are to be seated at their desks, not on the windowsill; and that *students* should cease conversing so that the *teacher* can begin her discussion. And yet over time, students and teachers (the principle actors in this social environment) may get to know one another fairly well. As this occurs, more of the complexity and uniqueness of each actor will begin to inform the student–teacher interactions. We may, therefore, hear the teacher say, "Okay, class, let's stand up and take our five-minute relaxation-stretch, which doesn't mean that we are going to start playing ninja warriors with Tommy, right Josh?" But, even with this change, what we see is that two rather distinct categories of persons (or actors) exist in the school classroom: teachers and students. And that each of the actors has rights and duties with respect to one another.

Now, if we think back over the time we spent in elementary school, it is likely that we can think of some teachers who were stricter than others, some who were nicer than others, and some from whom we learned more and found more interesting than others. And the same goes for our classmates. Some were very shy. Others were quite rambunctious. Some were eager to learn and to please the teacher, while others seemed ready to cause a little mischief whenever the opportunity presented itself. And perhaps, many exhibited a measure of each of these qualities at different times. But hopefully it is becoming clear that there is more to being an actor than a unique and complex person interacting with others. Interaction generally has a structure.

It is common for an individual to move through several different statuses over the course of a day. Think about how the status you occupy at any given time influences the nature of your social interactions. *(Shutterstock)*

The structure of interaction is organized around the respective statuses of the actors involved. Here, we are not referring to status in the sense of social prestige (i.e., the difference between a Supreme Court justice or the president of a university and someone who works as a dishwasher or cleans offices). Instead, we are referring to **status** as a recognized social position held by a person (or actor), such as teacher or student, parent or child, manager or employee. And these social positions tend to confer upon the actors involved unique sets of rights and duties that guide or provide a framework in which interaction can proceed. Sociologists generally refer to a person as holding a status and playing a role, with the **role** referring to the behaviors associated with a given status. Thus, "teacher" is a status, and teachers play certain expected roles. A teacher's role, may include being a disciplinarian, being a guide and mentor, grading homework in the evenings, being a colleague to one's peers, and so on. However, sociologists tend to simply refer to *roles* as shorthand for the *status-role complex*, a custom we will follow throughout much of the remainder of this book.

When I was a student (in elementary school and even in college), I always found it uncomfortable and strange to see my teacher out in public. After all, as far as I was concerned, her identity was "teacher"—nothing more, nothing less. And to see my teacher shopping for groceries, or out with her fiancée, or having a light-hearted conversation with a friend in a department store, upset my sense of how school, and my classroom, was ordered. But, if we think about it, most of us move through a typical day by sequencing (sometimes back and forth) through a series of statuses that provide a general structure to our interactions. In a typical day, I move from husband ("Good morning, Maria") to father ("Time to wake up for school son"), to teacher ("Today, class, we are going to discuss the elements of social structure"), to colleague ("We have to set a meeting with the department head for next Friday"), to customer ("How much for an oil change?"), and then back home to play husband and father again. In fact, over the course of our lives, we move through many different clusters of statuses. And, for any given phase in life, we refer to all of the statuses held by a person as that person's **status set**.

Furthermore, there are sets of generic or generalized statuses such as boy/girl, adult/child, African American/Hispanic American/Asian American, etc., which refer to gender, age, and race-ethnic statuses held by individuals. And these statuses often have implications for how someone is viewed by others within a range of more specified statuses that are more integral features of the person's formal interactional order. Depending upon the context, historical and otherwise, these statuses can have a pervasive impact upon a person's life, determining to a significant degree the kinds of statuses that person is permitted to hold, and shaping the nature of the statuses they do hold. In fact, social scientists have generally observed that highly traditional societies have been organized along age and sex categories and, based on these categories, strictly delineate the nature of the statuses that any individual may hold. Thus, a person's age and sex becomes a **master status**, or a social position having special significance for that individual's identity and course of life. In U.S. society, the women's movement has taken aim at gender—the cultural meaning and significance associated with being male or female—as a master status for women, which in times past has meant that educational and occupational opportunities for women were severely limited by the laws and customs of a society which consigned them to domestic roles and did not even permit them the political right to vote until early in the twentieth century. Race and ethnicity can also be viewed as a master status. African Americans were forcefully brought to this country as slaves, having virtually no rights. Even after slaves were freed at the end of the American Civil War, it took close to a century before the civil rights movement was successful in garnering the right to vote for African Americans in the American South.

We are assigned numerous social positions at birth (boy/girl, son/daughter, African American/Anglo American); others we acquire later in life (senior citizen). Each of these is an **ascribed status**, one that is assigned to us and over which we ultimately have little control. But many of the social positions that we come to occupy, first require that we put forth some effort, or demonstrate some degree of aptitude or ability, before we can adopt them. And these are reflective of **achieved status**, as their acquisition requires some ability or effort on our part. Making the volleyball team, getting a part in the school play, or landing your first job, are each examples of achieved status.

We must point out that any given status will likely not hold the same significance and meaning for every individual. Instead, individual actors inevitably differ in the value they place upon playing specific roles associated with a given status. For instance, imagine that during fourth grade you played in a youth soccer league on the weekends and took piano lessons two days a week after school. Also imagine that you absolutely loved playing on your soccer team, practiced with your friends whenever you had the chance, loved to wear your team shirt to school, and burst with pride whenever you scored a goal during a game. It seems likely that you were engaging in **role embracement**, or playing a role in a way that reflects, verifies and defines an important part of who you are, or your identity.

Now, imagine that you absolutely despised taking those piano lessons, and that when it came time to practice you would spend most of your time banging aggressively on the piano keys, repeatedly uttering just how "stupid" this whole activity was. And, when it came to your group piano lesson, you took on a demeanor of disinterest and relished any opportunity to clown around and make a mockery of the activities in which the class was engaged. In this instance, it seems likely that you were engaging in **role distance**, or a process by which you detached yourself from the role even as you engaged in it, signaling to yourself and others that this role is in no way closely aligned with the person you are (your identity). Keep in mind that most people vacillate between varying degrees of role distance or role embracement over time in any given role(s) that are associated with some status that they occupy. Continuing with our example about piano playing, consider what might happen when our fourth grader finds that she is invited to provide a mini-demonstration of what she has been learning on the piano during a family holiday event. If she receives a flurry of positive attention and social recognition from extended family, she may feel a sudden rush of pride and accomplishment and even some renewed motivation to continue with the lessons (role embracement).

Finally, we must acknowledge that both the way in which we approach or embrace our roles as well as the overarching manner in which those roles are constructed and related to other status-role complexes among the variety of actors in any given situation, has implications for the possible *forms of inter-action* that ensue. An extremely important form of interaction involves **coop-**

While our society places great emphasis upon competition and individual achievement, cooperation remains a core aspect of social life. *(Wikipedia)*

eration, where the interacting parties share the same mutually beneficial goal. The classroom situation requires a good measure of cooperation among teachers and students. For instance, students oftentimes must be quietly and attentively seated at their desks in order for the class to understand the lesson being presented by the teacher. Once a brief lesson is presented, teachers may oftentimes have students work cooperatively in groups to complete an exercise or experiment.

The classroom teacher may, at other times, initiate a **competition**, or a situation in which interacting parties struggle to attain some goal or reward not available to all, but do so within a clearly defined set of rules or norms. Such competitions may take the form of group quizzes, where students must compete to be the first to answer questions correctly, and doing so permits the winning individual or group to win some prize, say, candy. Later in life, as we move through the educational system, we come to realize how exams and grades represent an important source of competition. For those who have gone through the process of applying to college, high school grades and SAT exam scores are often important factors in determining who gets admitted to which schools.

Finally, we must consider a final form of interaction that may take place between individuals, groups, or even societies—a form of interaction that is inherently destructive. **Conflict** is a form of interaction in which the ends or goals of the interacting parties are in opposition. Here, depending upon the situation, force and/or violence may reign, and there is a clear sense that customary norms for interaction do not apply. At the societal level, war between nations or equivalent large entities would be the characteristic form of conflict. Here, death and destruction are unleashed, but there may be norms, even formal international agreements, that mitigate how the conflicting entities deal with civilian populations and military prisoners of war.

In everyday life, conflict between individuals or groups may not be so overt, all encompassing, and destructive. For instance, conflict may break out on the school playground, as disputes can emerge over which individuals or groups have control over valued resources such as the baseball field or the playground. This may lead to conflict that may involve physical altercations and/or bullying (which can involve physical and/or verbal abuse). When such conflicts do occur, there is a general and growing expectation that schools should not allow this form of interaction, and that school administrators should take formal action to reduce and eliminate it. Individual schools meet this expectation with varying degrees of success and cooperation from children and their families; moreover, children seem to find creative new ways to engage in conflict that falls beneath the normative radar of the school and its power to impose negative sanctions. While conflict in everyday life seems to persist in some areas, the shared value or ideal of creating a society in which overt and destructive conflict is minimized also persists.

Thus far, we have drawn upon examples to illustrate the building blocks of social structure by focusing on the domain of education, or the school. The next section will make clear how the educational system represents one element of a larger complex of social institutions. Social institutions represent key domains through which everyday life in society is organized, or structured, in systematic ways.

INSTITUTIONS

In the broadest sense, **institutions** are patterns of normative expectations that are applied widely to individuals and are backed up by sanctions (both positive and negative). In this broad sense, something as simple as a handshake can be an example of an institution. When someone extends a hand to you in greeting, that person has the backing of societal expectations that you will reciprocate. Not doing so, depending upon the situation, may reflect a serious breach of trust. This occurs because institutions—as patterns of normative expectations that are experienced in the immediacy of everyday interaction—are also informed by a more abstract set of values or ideals. On a certain level, U.S. society embraces the ideal that fellow citizens (and even noncitizen fellow human beings) share some measure of equality and that basic norms of decency and mutual respect inform human interaction. An effective ritual that symbolizes this is found in the simple handshake.

While handshakes and other general practices (folkways), which we regularly encounter without really giving them a second thought, form an important part of the institutional fabric of everyday life, our major focus in this book is on a larger set of institutional domains that make up key areas or arenas of social life. Here, we are talking about major social institutions in society, institutions that have distinctive goals, ends, or purposes (however imperfectly defined), and which consist of related clusters of normative expectations and comprise a distinctive set of interrelated statuses. The concept of the status/role complex, introduced earlier in this chapter, stipulates that statuses are often defined in interrelated pairs (such as teacher and student) and that these pairs are typically located within a given institutional setting—in this case, the educational system.

In the second half of this chapter, we will explore major social institutions that reflect key elements of the large scale social structures that make up society. These are the economic system, politics/government, family, religion, education, and the mass media. As we noted at the outset of our discussion (using the example of a simple handshake), institutions are primarily understood as clusters of normative expectations, but they are also informed by broader values and ideals. Sociologists contend that institutions both form and educate people. That is, they do not simply represent entities with which we must deal in order to achieve our own personal goals but are integral to the formation and shaping

By signifying a basic level of trust and goodwill between people, a simple handshake captures the power and significance of institutions in society. *(Wikipedia)*

of our individual goals, desires, hopes, and ambitions. Moreover, institutions shape the way individuals define themselves as part of larger entities, be they communities or society at large.

Economy represents an institutional domain wherein we secure, generate, transform, and distribute resources throughout society. The prevailing economic system here in the United States, and around the globe, is **capitalism**: an economic system in which goods and services are exchanged between buyers and sellers in a marketplace. Because of our strong cultural values emphasizing individual achievement and success, and the material comforts that come as rewards and symbols of that success, American style capitalism certainly has a powerful impact upon how we understand ourselves and our relationship to others as well as to the larger society. Among our deepest cultural beliefs is the belief in the power of the individual to forge of a life of his or her own through ambition and hard work, and that the impact of these personal actions, made possible by the capitalist system, will enhance the general welfare of society over time. In fact, the entrepreneur turned successful business owner holds a kind of mythical status in our culture. And yet, as we shall explore in later chapters, the entrepreneur represents only one aspect of our economic life, which in reality has come to be dominated by larger entities and systems reflective of the great corporations that today loom ever so large on the economic scene. That landscape has increasingly moved beyond the national to the global scene, and we have increasingly become concerned with the economic risks and uncertainties that we individually and collectively now confront on this larger stage. We have also been reminded over recent years of how vast corporate entities, while essential for generating and distributing the vast resources required by modern society, also have the potential to place the system at risk of financial collapse and/or environmental disaster.

In addition to an economic system that unleashes the power of individuals—and increasingly corporations—to pursue their own narrow economic interests, the social institution of **politics and government** reflects the need to establish collective goals and priorities as a society, and then to mobilize resources in order to achieve those ends. The United States is a **representative democracy**, wherein we exercise rights and duties as citizens by electing representatives to independent ruling bodies (such as the U.S. House of Representatives, the U.S. Senate, as well as their parallel bodies in state government, along with a host of local officials who represent us in our cities, towns, villages and counties), which in turn are charged with carrying out the will of the people for a specific period of time (typically two, four, or six years). One major source of political conflict is in defining the relationship between the government and the economy. This relationship is reflected in our shared ideals of freedom and justice, and the conflict manifests itself in debates about how we best secure and advance these ideals. We must also keep in mind that a central feature of these debates is focused on just how these ideals can and should best be defined. In subsequent chapters, we will emphasize how the historical growth of government over the past century is closely linked to the transformation of the United States from a largely agrarian society (rooted in farming or agriculture) to one that has become largely industrial and urban. With this shift a transformation has occurred in capitalist markets whereby local or regional markets have been gradually replaced by larger national and international markets. What this great transformation means is that individuals, families, and local communities find that their economic fates have become increasingly tied to forces beyond their local control, and so government institutions have emerged to help protect society against the large scale economic risks that accompany the opportunities that emerge with a large scale and productive economy. Also of central interest to us is the role of the government (through the military, the police, and other related entities) in protecting the population both from internal and external threats and enhancing the security and stability of the social order, all the while maintaining cherished freedoms.

In contrast to the economy, which is fueled by the competitive spirit in American culture, the **family** (here we also include friendship) represents a social institution in which cooperation and caring for others are defining features. In a historical context, this has included a focus on the bearing and raising of children and caring for elderly family members. Yet, the meaning of family has been contested and debated over recent decades. One significant abiding cultural ideal has been the heterosexual nuclear family, consisting of a husband and wife, along with their children. More recently, this type of nuclear family has diversified to include what has become an increasingly common pattern of single-parent (typically a mother) families with children. Furthermore, increasing numbers of adults actively choose not to marry and/or have children (or find themselves in this life situation), and with the high divorce rate (roughly four in ten marriages end in divorce), many families are remade and transformed in multiple ways. Family sociologist Andrew Cherlin speaks of two parallel notions of family that have emerged in our contemporary society and that somewhat uneasily co-exist. In his work, *Public and Private Families*, Cherlin notes how we still retain (on some level) a public notion of family, which involves understandings that relate family to the basic needs or requirements of the larger society—that is, that families exist to care for those who are vulnerable and dependent, namely children and the frail elderly. But, Cherlin also notes how private (and decidedly different) notions of family have become important to people over recent decades. These private notions characterize relationships whose major focus is on intimacy, which may or may not involve children, in which couples assume a relationship will last indefinitely, share a household, and pool their resources (to a significant degree). The key focus here is on intimacy as a fundamental glue that binds couples in relationships.

You may well wonder, "Who defines family?" Well, in one sense we all do, as expressed by the kind of commitments we make to others over the course of our lives. And yet, there are also formal legal considerations that define key dimensions of the limits and possibilities for this institution. Ongoing political debates about gay marriage and/or domestic partnerships have serious implications, particularly with respect to rights and privileges as well as benefits and resources currently enjoyed by heterosexual married couples. Will these rights and privileges be made available for those in same-sex unions? All in all, this complicated reality associated with the institution of family reflects the uncertainties associated with modern life as well as the potential for new and different models for the family institution. Most people, however, have a pretty strong sense about who is considered "family" and that family, in whatever light it is seen, is important.

Religion as an institution has also been undergoing dramatic shifts in ways that parallel the evolving institution of family. Here, the most significant shift is toward pluralization, a shift prompted by the growing diversity of faiths practiced in the United States as well as by the growing numbers of citizens for whom religion plays a greatly diminished or nonexistent role in life (a process known as **secularization**). Religion as social institution involves beliefs and practices centered on notions of the sacred or divine. For many, practicing a religion provides a sense of meaning and purpose in life, while at the same time setting limits and controls upon what is or is not acceptable behavior. In a contemporary world rooted in individualism and materialism, a world that is also beset with many uncertainties about the future, religion can provide the faithful with a sense of security and conviction, something stable and enduring in life. Many achieve this by joining **churches, mosques, or synagogues**, which are religious organizations that are integrated into the wider society. Others (particularly in recent decades) seek out the spiritual aspects of religion without the formal and organized qualities of a church. This movement, which likely represents the flip side of increasing secularization, is captured by the growing presence of New Age spirituality in American life. In general, however, the growing pluralization of religion forms an important context for debates about how boundaries between religion and state institutions are to be drawn. Another change, in addition to the growing pluralization and fragmentation of established and organized religion in society, is the significant role now played by other community and civic institutions (which also have an important historical role in U.S. society) that are educative or formative of the individual's character, and allow her to actualize cherished values and beliefs in relating to the larger world.

The rise and expansion of formal **education** over the last century has been a truly historic unprecedented development. In this book, we examine ongoing tensions surrounding the proper purpose of the educational system, some of which have sparked heated values debates, with one vision squarely focusing on education as preparation for work in the economy, and the other envisioning a larger role for the development of active and responsible citizenship. Our main focus is to highlight the enormous role that education in particular, and the growth and development of knowledge in general, plays in our advanced industrial society. Both concepts are central for defining the future in terms of prosperity and survival. In spite of this, our educational system is straining under the expectations placed upon it, as well as its general failure to serve vulnerable and marginalized populations, particularly in our inner cities, but also in remote and impoverished rural areas.

While the institution of the modern **mass media** generally falls under the purview of the economy, it has had a historical role as an institution of central importance for the preservation of democracy. Two themes of interest to us here are the enormous growth and corporate consolidation of the traditional mass media along with the rise of new media (blogs, newsgroups, Facebook, Google, etc.) and their implications for democracy. While mass media has served this traditional function of keeping the democratic public informed of news and political events of the day, its primary role seems to have become the promotion of consumption throughout the economy.

In the closing chapter(s) of this work, we examine the issue of the role of institutions and individuals in an emerging global context. What we explore here is the tension between those who understand institutions from one point of view of society (i.e., the U.S.-only view) versus the reality that societies are increasingly interconnected in a variety of ways. This disconnect in understanding affects how and whether institutions can properly serve their traditional functions. Many of the challenges and risks we confront as a society are really global in scope, with the most pressing among these being issues of natural resource exploitation and depletion, along with the question of achieving a sustainable global human–environmental ecosystem. Related to this, we examine the role of the individual/citizen (i.e., individual activities, identities, and commitments) in this emerging global verses national context.

ORGANIZATIONS

Many of our institutions have a high degree of formality, which of course includes a specialized purpose and unique sets of statuses and roles. However, the actual real-world manifestations of these generic entities called institutions, like the elementary school you attended in your hometown, tend to have certain characteristics in common. And here we don't simply mean comparing different schools to one another—we are also interested in comparing schools with government agencies and large businesses, to examine common patterns in how they operate. What we find is that many institutions are expressed in the real world as formal organizations. **Formal organizations** are large groups that are organized around a specific goal or purpose. And many formal organizations in the modern world take on the structure (more or less) of a **bureaucracy**, which is a complex organizational model that is focused on efficiency.

Bureaucracies are characterized by certain key characteristics or qualities. Foremost among these are a complex division of labor, a clear hierarchy of authority, formal rules and procedures, and of course, a focus on efficiency. Bureaucracy became the dominant organizational form both in government and business arenas over the past century or so, as society moved from being largely rural and agrarian to urban and industrial. With this shift, local markets grew into national and international ones, and business, along with the institutions of government, grew up along with them.

In some respects, we have a difficult time understanding just how dependent we have become upon bureaucratic organizations in the modern world. Bureaucracies support our everyday world in ways that we today take for granted. Those of us who live in cities can readily see how dependent we are upon the predictable delivery of goods and services that support our daily functioning. Among these goods and services are electricity, clean running water, sewer systems, waste removal, the maintenance of roads and other means of transportation, as well as the regular turnover of foodstuffs at our local supermarket chain, which ensures availability and freshness.

We are not simply dependent upon bureaucracy for the basic infrastructure and services that undergird and support our daily lives; we are also dependent on some of the underlying principles that define bureaucracy, and, as sociologist George Ritzer argues in *The McDonaldization of Society*, more and more aspects of the world around us are being organized around the principles of the fast-food restaurant. As Ritzer points out, chains are everywhere today, not simply in the fast-food arena. We may not at first recognize their resemblance to bureaucracy, but closer inspection shows us just how similar the principles that guide the operation of both are. Just pick up the phone and contact the customer service department of any major retail chain with which you do business, and you will most likely be greeted by an automated computerized voice answering service that asks you to make selections from a series predefined menu options.

Here, we want to introduce the concept of formal organizations, and with them the ideas of bureaucracy and McDonaldization. From this vantage point, we can better understand how our social institutions operate in practice. For instance, most Americans celebrate the innovation and creativity of the lone entrepreneur; in practice, however, our economy is dominated by large corporations, some having thousands of employees and billions of dollars in sales. These entities cannot help but be organized to a significant extent along bureaucratic lines, no matter how vociferously our business leaders may wish to deny this fact. The same anomaly exists in our perceptions about government. Government agencies are notoriously derided for being bureaucratic, unresponsive, and inefficient. But while Americans have always had an uneasy wariness of large government bureaucracies (with valid reasons), we have not found a way to make them go away. Moreover, if we were somehow able to make this happen, it is more than likely that we would want them—or more precisely, the services they provide—to come back.

Interestingly, the institution of family is probably the least formally and bureaucratically organized of all our major social institutions; it is, however, called upon to adapt to these formal organizations, particularly the workplace and the school, and organize family routines accordingly. Furthermore, parents confer resources upon their children. Some are material resources, such as clothing, computers, skate boards, etc., whereas others are social and cultural. With these latter resources, parents draw upon their own educational and cultural experiences, along with employment–career experiences to model and instruct how their children should navigate the organizational playing fields of life.

When it comes to religion, many churches have formal organizational structures, with the Catholic Church being perhaps the most powerful example. It is a global organization with a formal hierarchy, rules and regulations (policies and doctrines), and a complex division of labor. The U.S. educational system consists of thousands of local school districts, and most schools and school systems have a fundamental bureaucratic structure. This structure, which promotes efficiency and uniformity, is linked in important respects to principles of fairness and equal treatment. But unequal access to resources across school districts, instances of significant resource scarcity, and a growing awareness of the limitations and rigidities of bureaucracy, have led to numerous experiments with educational reform and numerous calls for dramatic changes and improvements.

Mass media is also subject to the power of bureaucracy. We have witnessed, for example, how many news organizations owned by large media corporations have come under increasing pressure to serve the profit motive rather than other goals once held in esteem. There has, for example, been increasing focus on cost cutting and a shift towards news being primarily entertainment, something that will attract viewers and advertising dollars. With the explosive growth in cable television over recent decades, this tendency has proliferated, with marketing and advertising targeting more and more people, including children.

A NOTE ON SOCIAL STRATIFICATION

Although this book focuses on social structure as it is manifested through social institutions and formal organizations, there is another important dimension of social structure that has dramatic implications for how the subject matter presented here must be understood. This other dimension is **social stratification,** which refers to how societies rank or privilege categories of people in a hierarchy. Recall our earlier discussion of how individual achievement and success (along with material comforts) are important values reinforced by U.S. society. There is an implicit assumption here that our social institutions support *all* individuals in their efforts to actualize these values to one degree or another. Now recall our discussion of ascribed, achieved, and especially, master status.

Historically, certain groups have been excluded from full and equal participation in some of our core societal institutions, a situation that can be directly related to social stratification. For instance, why was the women's movement essential? Its purpose was to advance women's participation in the realms of politics and the workplace (economy). This long struggle involved legal reform as well as major revisions in our cultural beliefs regarding women and their potential to participate in and contribute to society in ways that go well beyond domestic roles.

We can expand this illustration of social stratification by revisiting our discussion of how African Americans moved from a position of complete subjugation, to emancipation, and ultimately, to full political participation—with the caveat that this transformation did not come about in the South until the 1960s. Moreover, African Americans have also experienced discrimination in employment and housing, sometimes with the support of the legal system and formal government policies.

Social stratification has many faces and facets, all of which function in a way to treat members of a society unequally in various institutional domains. Among sociologists, the most common focus of this phenomenon has been along categories of race, social class, and gender, but stratification is in no way limited to these categories. Simply consider our discussion about the changing nature of family life and the ongoing debates surrounding the efforts of gay and lesbian couples to have their family status formally recognized by the state so that they might enjoy the full rights and benefits enjoyed by heterosexuals in their family relationships. Throughout this book, as we explore social structures in the form of formal institutions and organizations, we will also be pointing out the implications that these structures have for sustaining, exacerbating, or at times mitigating, social inequality—the backbone of the system of stratification in society.

Further Reading

Bellah. Robert N., Richard Madsen, William M. Sullivan, Ann Swidler, and Steven M. Tipton. *The Good Society*. New York: Alfred A. Knopf, 1991.

Cherlin, Andrew. *Public and Private Families: An Introduction*. 5th ed. Boston: McGraw-Hill, 2008.

Dobriner, William M. *Social Structures and Systems: A Sociological Overview*. Pacific Palisades, Calif.: Goodyear Publishing Company, 1969.

Macionis, John J. *Society: The Basics*. 10th ed. Upper Saddle River, N.J.: Prentice Hall, 2009.

Merton, Robert K. *Social Theory and Social Structure*. Glencoe: The Free Press, 1957.

Ritzer, George. *The McDonaldization of Society*: Thousand Oaks, Calif: Pine Forge/Sage, 1993.

CHAPTER 2

ORGANIZATIONS IN THE MODERN WORLD

Back of the factory system lies the household and neighborhood system. Those of us who are here today need go back only one, two or at most three generations to find a time when the household was practically the center in which were carried on, or about which were clustered, all of the typical forms of industrial occupation. . . . Instead of pressing a button and flooding the house with electric light, the whole process of getting illumination was followed in its toilsome length from the killing of the animal and the trying of the fat to the making of wicks and the dipping of candles. . . . The children, as they gained in strength and capacity, were gradually initiated into the mysteries of several processes. . . . In all this there was continual training of observation, of ingenuity, constructive imagination, of logical thought, and of the sense of reality acquired through first hand contact with actualities.

This observation, reproduced by Robert Bellah and his associates in *The Good Society*, was originally from *The School and Society*, written back in 1899 by John Dewey, the great American philosopher and educational reformer. How strikingly different are the images conveyed in this vignette from the one in our opening chapter about a student named Lisa who was entering college for the first time. In Lisa's world, our world really, education seems to take place in series of hermetically sealed environments, somewhat separated and cut off from the rest of life. In contrast, John Dewey was describing an earlier and predominantly agrarian world in which everyday life was a kind of classroom where the practical affairs of living were learned. But the classroom evoked by Dewey was a far cry from the familiar four walls inside of an isolated red brick building, where bells and buzzers signal the orderly movement from one subject matter to the next over the course of a fixed school day. Instead, it had a naturalistic and organic relationship to daily living.

How did we get from there to here? A sociological answer to that question is that we arrived via the great transformation to modernity along a pathway that dramatically altered the nature of the major social institutions that we today take for granted. This great transformation, brought about by processes of democratization, urbanization, and industrialization, involved new ways of organizing our world and the institutions of which it consists. It also introduced fundamental changes in our interactions with these institutions and with each other. In this chapter we first examine the great transformation to modernity as a prelude to exploring the nature of complex organizations in the modern world. For it is through complex organizations that our major social institutions take on form and structure in today's world.

THE GREAT TRANSFORMATION TO MODERNITY

The great transformation to modernity as it unfolded in the United States and Western Europe took place roughly during a time period stretching from the late 18th century into the early 20th century. In these two regions of the world increasingly unified nations emerged—nations that experienced, each at its own pace, growing industrial patterns of work and productive activity. These patterns were further impacted by urbanization, the movement of peoples from small towns and rural villages into cities, and by systems of democratic representation and forms of government that progressively incorporated ever widening segments of society into their fold.

The Industrial Revolution began in England with the invention of the steam engine by James Watt in 1765. Over the course of the next century, other Western European countries and the United States began following the same path. This transformation led to the gradual decline of agrarian forms of life in favor of a new industrial order.

Industrialization shifted the location, the organization, and the productive output of work in dramatic ways. In the preindustrial agrarian world, production of goods was generally carried out by craft workers on a small, labor-intensive scale. The work was typically done within the household. The Industrial Revolution involved a shift from small-scale, home-based production (sometimes referred to as **cottage work**) to work in factories that housed expensive but very productive machinery. Here groups of workers would carry out production as a larger, collective endeavor, organized by the owner of the factory. This typically involved breaking down the more complicated and numerous activities of the craft worker into a series of simple and repetitive routines carried out by a number of workers who formed part of an overall production system that was organized around the costly machinery. As the system evolved, an increasing proportion of the population began to work for wages in capitalist factories, as opposed to working for themselves on the family farm or in a skilled trade. With the rise of factory work new values emerged as the factory clock came to set the rhythms of daily life, eclipsing the sun and the seasons as arbiters of work schedules and punctuality.

As the factory system assumed an ever greater presence in society, it generated an enormous increase in the overall production of goods. It also led to the growth of cities, a phenomenon called **urbanization**, by bringing large numbers of people, accustomed to an agrarian way of life and the daily practices and habits appropriate to rural living, into crowded cities that were unprepared to accommodate the influx of thousands of newcomers. The urban centers grew haphazardly, with little if any planning. Basic public services were unavailable, except perhaps in more affluent districts that were generally segregated from the areas populated by the impoverished masses. Those who worked in the city's

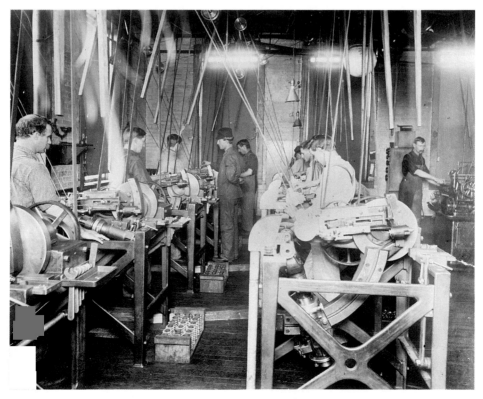

Industrialization dramatically transformed a preindustrial way of life by imposing the rhythms and patterns of the factory upon an agrarian-based population. *(Library of Congress)*

factories lived without functioning sewers, clean air, or clean water, in environments ripe for contagious diseases and epidemics.

Oftentimes, urbanization brought together diverse populations, people with different customs, beliefs and cultural backgrounds. This was the case in the United States during the late 19th century. As the country's great industrial transformation began to evolve, immigrants began to arrive, primarily from Europe. To this day, major U.S. cities have been prime destinations for groups of immigrants hailing from all corners of the globe, adding to, replenishing, and diversifying the nation's population.

Two events that occurred around the time of the great transformation to modernity were the American revolution (1776) and the French Revolution (1789). Each, in its own way, represented the birth of a democratic form of government. But in each of these countries, the growing pains of **democracy** extended well beyond these initial events. In some respects, we see similar growing pains today as humanity continues its uncertain movement toward democratic enfranchisement for all people, both at a societal level and at a global level.

Family in a tenement kitchen at the beginning of the 20th century. The growth of cities during industrialization often led to urban squalor, a result of insufficient planning and development. For the people who flocked to the cities to find work, there were few if any proper public services to ensure they had clean water, sanitation, and sewage disposal—all the public provisions that we take for granted today. *(Library of Congress)*

And yet, during the first half of the nineteenth century, the democracy that many in our contemporary world view in such a positive manner was viewed as a radical and threatening idea by many, especially in a Europe entrenched in a centuries' old system of government.

Early on, democracy had succeeded in unseating or weakening the power and privileges of kings and queens; the old feudal-aristocratic order gave way to a newly empowered **bourgeoisie**, a class consisting of small entrepreneurs (business owners), property owning landlords, and others who had experienced the heaviest burden of taxation. As democratic systems of government slowly or swiftly assumed their place in society, industrial capitalism emerged as the predominant economic system, and social movements aimed at the enfranchisement of wage laborers soon developed, particularly in England but also in other parts of Europe. These groups also wanted the **state** (that is, the government) to respond to their needs and to serve their interests in achieving security and material comfort in this new order.

THE GROWING PRESENCE OF SECONDARY GROUPS IN SOCIETY

As increasing numbers of people moved away from rural life and the stable social world to which their ancestors had been accustomed into new and more densely populated cities, with far more diverse populations, many social activists raised concerns about the breakdown and fragmentation of stable, traditional communities. Furthermore, the practice of wage labor had become the primary means by which newly urban working classes could make a living, and this system seemed far more impersonal, competitive, and alienating than the older social economy of an earlier time. In the new urban factories, workers experienced a great measure of social distance from their well-to-do employers, as wage labor, more or less, defined the extent of their relationship and obligations to one another. Unlike in smaller, more close-knit communities, there was little to bind the two classes together. Employers needed labor in their factories, and they paid workers to perform that labor. If an employer's need for labor disappeared, so would the relationship.

Workers had to adapt to an increasingly impersonal and competitive economic environment; they also began to interact with a wider range of people, lifestyles, and values. Socially aware observers of this paradigm shift began to notice and comment on the decline in importance of what has been referred to as the **primary group** in society. One such observer was American sociologist Charles H. Cooley, who lived and wrote around the turn of the twentieth century.

In his work, *Social Organization*, Cooley explored **primary groups**, which he viewed as small and intimate, organized around face-to-face relationships, and having a common spirit—a sense of a "we" feeling among members of the group. This feeling, according to Cooley, was generated by close and continuous

Charles Cooley considered the primary group as morally good. From this perspective, like many social critics of his time, he raised concerns about the impersonal and competitive nature of industrial urban society. Today, much of our time is spent in secondary group contexts, interacting with people with whom we may have limited personal involvement and personal understanding. The occasional family reunion reminds us of this reality. *(Shutterstock)*

interaction and by affect (emotion) over a long period of time, leading to a merging of the self with the common life and aims of the group. Cooley argued that regardless of culture, society, or historical setting, the primary group is of fundamental import in forming the character and ideals of the individual. Relevant here are groups such as extended family, close friendships, and community. Belonging to such groups, an individual living in a preindustrial world could very well experience pervasive and continuous involvement over the course of a lifetime. Given that Cooley viewed primary groups as the central unit of social life and organization in society, it is easy to understand his concerns about the impersonal qualities of the industrial order burgeoning around him.

As an increasingly industrial-urban society has evolved, so has the presence and significance of the secondary group in society. **Secondary groups** are typically far larger in size than primary groups and tend to be organized around a specific goal or purpose rather than an open-ended and diffuse range of goals and purposes. They are structured in such a way that the relationships between individuals are more distant and impersonal, involving a greater degree of competition than exists in primary groups, which have a more cooperative framework. Finally, secondary groups are more formal in that obligations, involvements, rights, duties, rewards, and punishments are more clearly and explicitly defined for members. Building on our school example, we can easily illustrate this point: classes that have very specific meeting times, routine evaluations for completing homework and taking exams (with the assumption that all students will be evaluated in a uniform and consistent manner). Students may try out for the volleyball team or the school marching band and have to demonstrate their talents before being admitted into the group. Extrapolating from the school setting to the workplace setting (because sooner or later, almost everyone has to work for a living), would-be employees must formally apply for a job. If hired, they must then take on a set of duties for a specified hourly wage, clocking in and out at the prescribed times as required by the terms of employment.

THE RATIONALIZATION OF SOCIETY

Very much in line with our discussion of the great transformation to modernity (characterized by urbanization, industrialization, democracy, and an emphasis on secondary groups), is the notion of an increasing **rationalization** of society. This idea of societal rationalization was a construct introduced by classical sociologist Max Weber, an early 20th-century German scholar who did much to establish sociology as a scientific discipline. A major work of Weber's that explores the theme of societal rationalization is *The Protestant Ethic and the Spirit of Capitalism*. In this book and in his other important works, Weber envisioned a long historical process of societal rationalization, which would eventually encompass and have a profound effect on all spheres of life, including religion, law, politics, scientific exploration, and even culture and the arts. Central to this process is a shift in how people understand and approach their world.

Weber envisioned that everyday life, once defined by folk beliefs and practices and filled with religious understandings, had increasingly come under the sway of secular influences that subjected life to rational scientific calculation. Under such influences, according to Weber, the systematic advance of scientific knowledge would eventually uncover, examine, and assess all aspects of everyday life, and bring it under rational control. First and foremost in this paradigm was capitalism, a fiercely competitive economic system that encouraged a scientific worldview as the development of new and advanced technologies were becoming ever more essential as a means of advancing productivity throughout the factory system. Over time this new rational worldview had increasingly become the common sense way to approach everyday affairs in virtually all spheres of life.

Rationality and Types of Social Action

Max Weber was fascinated with this new **rational life orientation.** To better understand its growth and development, he compared it with other general approaches to behavior in the social world that were predominant in varying degrees in a range of societies and historical contexts. The first of these approaches he termed **means-end**, which is reflective of this rational life orientation (and of rationalization in general). To embrace means-end rationality involves viewing other people (as well as all aspects of our material world) as means to our own rationally calculated ends or goals. The burgeoning capitalist enterprises of Weber's era provide the clearest examples of this type of life orientation. In this milieu, the owner of a business (say a factory) is compelled to view employees (human beings) as a source of labor, a cost involved in producing a product. The employees are thus viewed in precisely the same manner as are all of the raw material inputs (be they steel, leather, wood, glass) that are involved in the production process. Therefore, should our factory owner find a less expensive substitute (given comparable quality) for some human or raw material input into the production process, he would be compelled to replace the original with this lower cost substitute, because doing so would advance his narrowly defined goal or purpose—that is, profitability.

Weber identified several types of social action, but two others are of interest to us in this discussion: value rational and traditional. With **value rational** social action, some ethical (moral) or religious value is consciously embraced for its own sake, thus directing individuals in their interactions with others and the world around them. Take a principle such as the Golden Rule ("Do unto others as you would have them do unto you"). This rule can take on a purely ethical or a religious interpretation. One who fully embraces this principle treats others accordingly, even though these others may not reciprocate and may reject the principle even as they enjoy the benefits it bestows upon them.

Traditional social action refers to those behaviors and interactions that are defined by habit or custom, which has typically been followed over a long period of time and which (often unquestioned) defines the practices the individual engages in. Weber placed special emphasis on traditional forms of social action, as he deemed these to be the most resistant to change throughout world history. A major interest of Weber's lay in how capitalism emerged in Western Europe in spite of resistance from an agrarian peasantry with lives rooted in local custom and religious practices. In connection with this (and similar seemingly contradictory phenomena), Weber understood the modern world as a world in which the forces of tradition had been overcome by means-end social action and overall societal rationalization. Nevertheless, Weber strongly emphasized that human action likely involves a blending of at least some of these types of social action and is only rarely characterized by one pure type. His main point, however, was to illustrate how different types of social action can grow in significance and thereby redirect an individual's general life orientation in a new direction.

The Protestant Ethic

Throughout history, Weber argues, religion often strongly reinforced value rational, but even more so, traditional orientations, to social action. He noted that religion had generally acted as a resistant barrier to new and innovative forms of social action. In contrast to this generalization, however, Weber painstakingly delineated how the overall cultural influence of Protestantism was to provide support for societal rationalization in general and rational capitalism in particular.

In his major work on the Protestant ethic and the spirit of capitalism, Weber noted how European Protestants took great interest in business and commerce, while Catholics were more inclined to embrace the traditional customs and practices. Furthermore, Protestants were more inclined to embrace principles that Weber identified as emblematic of a capitalist ethos or spirit. This ethic is captured by such aphorisms as "time is money," and "early to bed, early to rise, makes a man healthy, wealthy, and wise," sayings that are still familiar to us today. In highlighting these sayings and the ideas behind them, Weber drew on the writings of a great 18th-century American, Ben Franklin, who understood how very useful and practical such principles were for achieving success in the emergent capitalist system.

The details of Weber's examination of the cultural evolution and wider influence of Protestant Christianity extend far beyond our immediate interests here. However, his thesis points to how these Protestant Christians, concerned about their ultimate fates, came to embrace material wealth as an outward sign that they were destined to receive God's blessings. This understanding reinforced a growing notion about the importance of working tirelessly in a *calling* (career) and had a powerful effect on the believer and his inner life. The focus of a person's life shifted toward an ascetic and self-disciplined devotion to productive work, which came to be understood as an expression of spiritual virtue. Weber envisioned this as a powerful cultural force that resonated with rational industrial capitalism.

Weber pointed out that this ascetic Protestantism was far more compatible with capitalism than was the traditional Catholicism of the preindustrial world, which views the acquisition of wealth as potentially detrimental to one's salvation. Catholic sensibilities were formed out of wider teachings urging the renunciation of wealth in favor of charitable giving to the poor. In the end, Weber's view was that a Protestant ethic may have aided and abetted the triumph of rational capitalism, but once this was achieved the religious supports that promoted it were no longer necessary. Rationalization would gradually pull humanity into its orbit—believers and nonbelievers alike—and would set its own terms and conditions for the world we were destined to inhabit.

Rationality-Legal Authority and Modern Democracy

As was noted earlier in this chapter, one key development in the transition to modernity was the rise of democratic systems of government. Weber was especially interested in democratization as part of an overall rationalization process. And while he noted that the possibility for direct political participation among the citizenry would be limited with the growth of large nation states, he envisioned their indirect participation through representative forms of government (democracy) in which elected officials are granted wide decision-making authority by the populace.

With modernity and democracy, a new form of political rule was established, a form Weber called **rational-legal authority**. Under this system, elected officials owe their obedience to what is commonly referred to as the **rule of law**. This means that formally enacted legal rules define the nature of the electoral process and the nature and degree of decision-making authority granted to elected officials. In the end, officials maintain the consent of the governed by operating within the legally defined boundaries that circumscribe their positions. Weber contrasted this type of authority with forms that were more typically found in earlier times. One such form he labeled "traditional authority," and it was this form that characterized political rule in Europe under the feudal system, which eventually gave way to capitalism. In this earlier context, **traditional authority** literally meant that the sanctity of tradition defined who could legitimately rule a territory, and in this context, rule was assumed by monarchs (kings and queens) and nobles, with authority passing down through male heirs based upon the bloodlines of the ruling aristocracy.

While traditional authority involved a somewhat haphazard and informal system of administration, with monarchs granting authority to trusted and loyal advisors, the emergence of rational-legal authority witnessed the rise of a far more rational and efficient system of administration. Under this system, Weber noted, modern forms of governing required large administrative staffs with a wide range of formally trained technical experts accorded a good measure of latitude to carry out their duties. Loyalty in this context is, in principle, not to be given to the elected official (or to the monarch, as would have been expected under traditional authority), but instead to the legally defined parameters of the administrative position. According to Weber, under rational-legal authority, the administrative apparatus achieved powers, capabilities, and a degree of efficiency unparalleled in earlier times, especially as it existed under traditional forms of authority. However, this powerful administrative apparatus was not without cost to the overall democratic process. The knowledge, experience, and discretion

Queen Elizabeth II. The United Kingdom retains vestiges of traditional authority by maintaining a constitutional monarchy. Under this system, a member of the royal family serves as nominal head of state, but performs functions and duties separate from party politics and actual governing. *(Wikipedia)*

assumed by technical experts served to remove many aspects of the process of governing from the immediate understandings of everyday citizens. The organizational model through which rational-legal authority came to be exercised was viewed by Weber as the ultimate manifestation of the rationalization process. And it is to this model, bureaucracy, that we now turn.

BUREAUCRACY

While bureaucracy became essential for the legitimate administration of government activity under the rational-legal system of democracy, it was also an essential element in the rise of the modern industrial economy. We normally associate machine production with the industrial economy, but the operations of business organizations were also rationalized, with a focus on precision, speed, and efficient use of human and nonhuman resources. Together the factory system and the rationalized business organization emerged as essential elements of the capitalist system. In fact, Weber envisioned the organized bureaucracy (whether it be in a business or government context) as a kind of machine—its human workforce serving as so many cogs, continuously processing its primary input, an endless stream of paperwork (files), which today is increasingly created and preserved in electronic form.

The imagery of a machine made up of human cogs is not far off from the reality of a bureaucratic model of organization. This model has several key elements. First, is a **hierarchy of authority**, meaning there is a clear chain of command that defines the levels of decision-making authority present throughout the organization. As we move toward the top of the organizational hierarchy (or chart) we find that individuals (and their offices or departments) tend to have increasingly greater levels of decision-making authority. Those with higher levels of authority often delegate responsibility to individuals at lower levels, and so on—when questions emerge about a proper policy or decision, they move up the chain of command until a final decision is made. Along similar lines, disagreements at lower levels of the organization move up the chain of command until they are satisfactorily resolved.

Next, we have a high degree of **specialization** that is part of a *complex division of labor*. The mission carried out by any bureaucracy is translated into a narrower set of goals and objectives that are carried out by breaking down and dividing up the work that needs to be accomplished into a series of smaller specialized tasks to be performed by specialized offices or departments, and the personnel within them. Throughout any bureaucratic organization will be a range of **technical-professional experts**, who receive specialized training in their defined area of expertise, and in the recent past, were likely to forge long-term careers with organizations that employed them. These experts are recruited by organizations and evaluated over time based upon a set of formal-technical criteria (in earlier times, particularly under forms of traditional authority, the emphasis may have been more on loyalty and family affiliations than on skill sets). The great advance of scientific knowledge and the vast expansion of the formal system of education over the past century, along with the enormous growth of universities, are a testament to Weber's image of the modern rational era as one that was to witness the rise of specialized forms of knowledge, science in general, and the professional-technical expert.

Just as the machinery in a factory is operated to produce large quantities of a uniformly consistent product, so does the bureaucracy seek to operate in a predictable and systematic fashion, which it achieves though an extensive set of **rules and regulations**. With these in place, the organization explicitly defines all aspects of its operation, and processes the files and its clients in a clear and consistent manner. In order for the rules and regulations to be applied such that the bureaucracy operates in a smooth and predictable manner, its personnel must act and treat clients in an **impersonal** manner. In fact, Weber noted that this requires that the bureaucrat functions without hatred, passion, affection, or enthusiasm in carrying out his duty to the organization. This impersonality need not be interpreted as rudeness, although that might at times be the case, but it requires that clients be treated as *cases*, and therefore, not given special treatment, nor should they be denied fair treatment. In the end, bureaucratic fairness, or impersonality, means applying the rules and regulations in a fair and uniform manner, as they have been defined by the organization.

As noted above, clients are ideally to be treated as cases by the bureaucracy— not subject to prejudice, discrimination, or favoritism. Instead, the bureaucrat is to be concerned only with the client's file, or the paperwork, which is the focus of

Max Weber noted that bureaucratic fairness depended upon conducting business on an impersonal level, meaning that bureaucrats treat their clients as cases and do not allow prejudice or favoritism to enter into their professional judgment. He also realized how the growing bureaucratic context of modern life could lead people to feel alienated from society. *(Shutterstock)*

his impersonal application of the organization's rules and regulations. The sum total of these principles or elements of bureaucracy add up to a larger system of rules and operating principles that are geared toward the efficient achievement of the organization's explicitly defined goals. The efficiency is realized by this larger systemic organization of personnel along with the organization's highly formalized rules and procedures, once again reflecting a system that functions much like a machine.

Finally, as we all have probably experienced in our own lives, as bureaucracies expand and grow more complex and as our society increasingly functions through the mechanisms of bureaucracy, all manner of problems emerge. Many organizations get bogged down with **red tape**, the endless accumulation of rules and regulations, that can confuse, frustrate, and demoralize both the organization's personnel and its clients. This (and similar problems) seems to characterize the rise of bureaucracy in modern society. At the same time, it has made possible an enormous growth in societal affluence and has enabled a reasonably comfortable urban industrial way of life. Weber envisioned that rationalization and bureaucracy would advance and envelope increasing areas of modern economic, social, and cultural life, creating what he called an *iron cage* in which we moderns would be destined to live. Furthermore, he envisioned this as a bargain that made the modern world possible. It is a world that few of us would willingly leave behind, but the bargain grows increasingly more difficult to sustain.

TYPES OF ORGANIZATIONS

It should be clear from our discussion that the role of bureaucracy in the modern world is increasing; it remains to be clarified just what it is that is bureaucratized. Recall the earlier discussion of secondary groups and their core characteristics. Secondary groups are large and typically impersonal; they demand short-term or intermittent involvement from their members; they have a competitive (versus cooperative) orientation; and they are organized around a specific goal or purpose. If we add to these characteristics a conscious effort at coordination and control directed in an ongoing manner, we have a reasonably working definition of a **formal organization.** Many sociologists, and certainly many inspired by Weber, liken our contemporary world to a society of organizations.

Sociologist Amitai Etzioni has provided the field with a simplified but highly useful framework for identifying key types of organizations. He identifies three basic types which are distinguished primarily on the basis of why people participate in them as well as on the types of managerial controls that are used to ensure that members act in a manner that serves the organization's goals. The first type, **utilitarian**, is fundamentally organized around profit making. For employees, this involves making a wage or a salary, all of which takes place primarily in the capitalist marketplace. Thus, if your parents work for a living, and bring home a paycheck every couple of weeks, or if they run a small busi-

Normative organizations channel energy and commitment of their members toward morally worthwhile goals. Here, the American Red Cross volunteers are helping Minnesota residents after a flood. *(Wikipedia)*

ness, they are invariably working within utilitarian organizations. Businesses like Microsoft, Nike, Ford, Google, McDonald's, American Eagle, and ESPN are all utilitarian organizations. Perhaps you currently hold a part-time job with a utilitarian organization. If so, you likely would end your participation with this organization if the people in charge decided to stop paying your wages.

Normative organizations are distinguished by their mission and goals. People tend to join or participate in them because they believe that the organization is doing something good, admirable, and morally worthwhile. *Voluntary associations* such as the Red Cross, UNICEF, Big Brothers and Big Sisters, and the Boys and Girls Clubs of America, are normative organizations. They often depend upon individuals to volunteer their time (or contribute some of their money) without any expectation of direct material or monetary compensation or reward. Many young adults find that doing volunteer work is a satisfying endeavor, because it makes them feel connected to others and feel good about themselves as they help make their community or the world a better place. Other types of normative organizations include churches and political parties. The key being, once again, a defined mission or goal that draws upon members' moral commitments and directs their energies and enthusiasm toward the accomplishment of worthwhile endeavors.

Finally, there are organizations that must rely upon force or coercion to motivate, direct, and control the actions of their members. Membership in a **coercive organization** is involuntary, and typical examples of these organizations would be prisons or psychiatric hospitals. In such organizations, great efforts are placed upon maintaining organizational boundaries, literally keeping the members in. Bars, locks, fences, and security personnel are common features of a coercive organization.

We should have a general awareness of these differing types of organizations because they have significant implications in our world. Understanding how managers run and operate them (including the kinds of incentives they believe will motivate the organization's members) and how members, in turn, are motivated to give of themselves and direct their energies towards the accomplishment of the organization's goals helps us to understand the greater society in which these organizations function and which these organizations shape. We must also be mindful that the characteristics provided here are general and do not necessary reflect the motivations of each and every member. For instance, a prison supervisor has different motivations (utilitarian) that influence his participation from those of the prisoners (coercive) under his watch. To provide one final example, I'll draw on real-world experience. Whenever I teach my university students about the different types of organizations, several invariably ask whether the school system is a coercive organization. The question arises because many students feel that school attendance is forced by rule of law. Or they might ask about a parent who hates his job but has to put food on the table for the family? Does this make the organization that offers the job and pay the salary a coercive organization? Such questions make one appreciate the variegated motives held by members of all large organization; they also underscore how those who are called to manage these entities must take these and similar questions into account in their efforts to achieve their organizations' goals.

THE PATTERN VARIABLES

Thus far in this chapter, we have looked at how life in the modern industrial world is accompanied by an increasingly rationalized approach to social action. We introduced the rise in significance of means-end social action and the increasing role played by secondary groups in the lives of individuals. We have also discussed how the Protestant ethic left its stamp on the developing spirit of capitalism. Building upon these and related themes, Talcott Parsons (arguably the preeminent American sociologist of the 20th century) developed a schema to help us understand general orientations to social action in our modern industrial world, in contrast to the preindustrial world, especially those orientations characterized by strong and tradition-minded kinship and community structures. Parsons referred to this schema as the **pattern variables**, variables that reflect decisions that human actors must make in orienting their behaviors in various social situations, before taking some course of action. Now, for those of us who have come of age in the modern industrial world, these decisions generally become a part of our "taken for granted" understanding about how our world operates.

Parsons's theory or schema regarding social action involves several elements or variables around which social action is organized. These pattern variables were developed in pairs to reflect general behavioral orientations characteristic of either traditional (preindustrial) or modern (industrial) societies. Parsons labeled traditional preindustrial societies as *expressive* and modern industrial societies as *instrumental*. He also developed five pattern variable pairings that would serve to frame an understanding of how any social actor becomes orientated toward a specific behavior pattern in any given situation.

The first pair that Parsons defined was **ascription** (traditional) versus **achievement** (modern). Here the idea is that the actor (or person) can orient behavior toward self and others on the basis of ascribed characteristics such as age, gender, race/ethnicity, even religion, or on the basis of what the actor has done or has demonstrated that he or she is capable of doing (achieved). Certainly when you apply for a job or pursue a career one day, you should expect that your educational preparation and wider experiences (achievements) will be taken into account by a potential employer and that far more attention will be given to these things than to your age, gender, or race/ethnic background (ascription). In fact, the legal system has evolved to reflect this expectation by making certain related forms of discrimination illegal. We also know, however, that there are other situations where ascription plays a far more significant role in how actors define situations. For instance, we sort many of our school-based organized sports teams by age and often gender—although this has also been changing somewhat to reflect emerging values and ideals. All this considered, we can be reasonably certain that a high school boy would not be allowed to play on his much younger sister's elementary school soccer team.

A second pattern variable revolves around **diffuseness** (traditional) versus **specificity** (modern). Today, many of the formal roles we carry out involve a very narrow or highly specific range of demands. For instance, in the college/university setting, the obligations that students and their instructors have toward one another are normally spelled out in the course syllabus, which may involve attending class only during the time periods prescribed by the university course schedule, as well as such duties as homework, papers, and exams. However, you should not expect your professor to ask you to help him rake his lawn on the weekend or babysit his children. Contrast such a highly specified relationship with one you may have with a very close and long-term friend or family member, where you may walk to school together, spend time playing video games on the weekends, go on vacation together, and help one another move into a new apartment. Such relationships involve a diffuse or highly varied range of demands.

Continuing with our example, a third pair of pattern variables reflects **affectivity** (traditional) versus **affective neutrality** (modern). Affect refers to feeling, and Parsons intended these pattern variables to reflect whether one could expect emotional gratification from a relationship. Certainly, we are expected to respond with a deep sense of empathy and emotion to the triumphs and tragedies, the achievements and disappointments, of those whom we consider close friends or family. In contrast, while we do not want our professors to behave like robots, we also know that too much emotional expression and intimacy on the part of professors toward some of their students (and vice versa) may be viewed with suspicion by other students as well as by administrators and colleagues, sometimes even leading to formal sanctions being applied by the institution.

A fourth pattern variable involves **particularism** (traditional) versus **universalism** (modern). The behavioral orientation here involves whether to base one's actions upon a particular and personal relationship with another or to base one's actions on a universal set of standards or criteria. If the basketball coach's son is playing on the team, should the son automatically become a starter due to his favored status with the father, or should the coach apply a universal standard of performance and make an impersonal evaluation as to whether his son deserves a spot on the team? Many coaches in such situations decide to apply a slightly higher (universal) standard in evaluating their own sons or daughters, just to preclude any charges of favoritism (particularism). This principle of universalism, coupled with achievement (versus ascription), is a cornerstone of our professed beliefs and values regarding equal opportunity in employment throughout U.S. society.

A final pattern variable involves the distinction between **collectivity** (traditional) and **self** (modern). Modern American mainstream culture is engrained with a self-orientation. Parents, for example, often encourage their children to demonstrate individual achievement in their academic schoolwork and in their extracurricular activities. A good example of a more collective orientation comes from the movie *My Big Fat Greek Wedding*, where a young adult woman struggles to find time apart from her extended family so that she can take some college courses. Doing so, however, means that she would no longer have the time to gather with her cousins and aunts every afternoon at their family-owned diner, and she realizes that taking such action would be viewed as extremely selfish. In the end, by offering to take some business courses that would enable her to help with her aunt's travel agency, she gains support from her family. Back to the collective!

These five pattern variables help us understand the behavioral continuum laid out by Parsons. Through these and the other approaches we have explored ways that help us understand the shifting focus and orientations to social action in the modern world and have hopefully developed a clearer sense of how our behavior is very broadly framed (but never fully determined) as we take on roles as actors in a range of institutional settings.

LOOKING AHEAD

In the following chapter, we will continue to draw upon Weber's ideas regarding growing rationalization and bureaucracy in the modern world. We will also explore how a related set of principles (based on the ideas of F. W. Taylor and Henry Ford) have driven the evolution of manufacturing and production operations in factories throughout much of the twentieth century. With these in mind, we will also explore a new phenomenon called McDonaldization, which is rooted in these earlier principles and now represents a powerful organizational force shaping and rationalizing ever-expanding dimensions of our contemporary world.

Further Reading

Bellah. Robert N., Richard Madsen, William M. Sullivan, Ann Swidler, and Steven M. Tipton. *The Good Society.* New York: Alfred A. Knopf, 1991.

Bratton, John, David Denham, and Linda Deutschmann. *Capitalism and Classical Sociological Theory.* Toronto: University of Toronto Press, 2009.

Cooley, Charles H. *Human Nature and the Social Order.* New York: Scribner's, 1922.

Kivisto, Peter. *Key Ideas in Sociology.* 2nd ed. Thousand Oaks, Calif.: Pine Forge, 2004.

Macionis, John J. *Society: The Basics.* 10th ed. Upper Saddle River, N.J.: Prentice Hall, 2009.

Parsons, Talcott. *Toward a General Theory of Action.* Edward A. Shils and T. Parsons (Eds.). Cambridge, Mass.: Harvard University Press, 1951.

Ritzer, George. *The McDonaldization of Society*: Thousand Oaks, Calif.: Pine Forge/Sage, 1993.

Weber, Max. *The Protestant Ethic and the Spirit of Capitalism.* London: Harper Collins Academic, [1904–1905] 1930.

CHAPTER 3

THE McDONALDIZATION OF SOCIETY

We have found out . . . that we cannot trust some people who are nonconformists . . . We will make conformists out of them in a hurry . . . The organization cannot trust the individual; the individual must trust the organization.

The quote that opens this chapter, cited in Eric Schlosser's bestselling book *Fast Food Nation*, is from none other than Ray Kroc, the man who successfully transformed McDonald's into a nationwide and then a worldwide franchise. In the book, which also references several other fast-food franchises that have become touchstones throughout our cultural landscape (Dunkin' Donuts, Taco Bell, Wendy's, Domino's, and Kentucky Fried Chicken), Schlosser points out with a great sense of irony how the fast-food industry's founding fathers learned early on that the key to successfully franchising a fast-food restaurant was uniformity. And yet, he explains, these same entrepreneurs were mostly unconventional noncomformists—too ambitious, creative, and driven to ever fit neatly within the kinds of organizations alluded to in the quote from Ray Kroc. Nonetheless, their collective business success, widely celebrated as part of our own distinctly American folklore, has had a tremendous homogenizing effect on our social, cultural, and physical, landscape.

It is easy to take for granted or simply fail to notice how much of American life and culture looks, feels, and is experienced in the same way. In my normal everyday travels around town, including the 7 miles I drive to and from work, for example, I pass at least five McDonald's restaurants. But at every shopping

Raymond A. Kroc eating a hamburger in front of a McDonald's. Early fast-food entrepreneurs helped spark a transformation in America's commercial and cultural landscape. While we celebrate their drive, talent, and creativity, some argue that an unintentional consequence of their collective triumph has been increased uniformity and organizational control. *(Getty)*

mall or strip mall, I can also see an endless array of other familiar retail chains and franchises: Starbucks, the Gap and American Eagle, Firestone and Jiffy Lube, Best Buy, and Home Depot, all of which attest to Schlosser's premise that "the basic thinking behind fast food has become the operating system of today's retail economy, wiping out small businesses, obliterating regional differences, and spreading identical stores throughout the country like a self-replicating code." By now, this transformation is now pretty much complete. In fact, many of us know of no other world besides the one dominated by these endless retail chains and franchises. They represent the world in which we have been incubating and which makes us comfortably (or uneasily) familiar with a wide array of homogenized choices.

F.W. TAYLOR AND THE RISE OF SCIENTIFIC MANAGEMENT
So how did we make the leap from Weber's bureaucracy to McDonald's? It's not hard to see that both are highly rationalized, but it is also rather obvious that they emerged from different spheres or organizational concerns. We can certainly think of both as products of a broader movement towards rational capitalism, but the fast-food franchise can best be understood as an outgrowth of developments in production and manufacturing, part of the outgrowth of the great transformation to modernity, which we call the Industrial Revolution.

Earlier in this text we described the Industrial Revolution as a movement that shifted the location, the organization, and the productive output of work in dramatic ways. It moved the work (and the workforce) from small-scale home-based production to big factories with expensive but very productive machinery. Independent craftsmen gave way to wage laborers hired by factory owners to carry out large-scale production. New values emerged, and the rhythms of daily life came to be increasingly synchronized with the factory clock. Included in (and sometimes propelling) this movement were urbanization and democratic forms of government.

The early twentieth century saw another set of historical changes, something we call the a **second wave in the great Industrial Revolution**. If the first wave was associated with the development of machine technology, the second wave was focused on adjusting the workforce and the rhythms of industrial work to meet the demanding pace and enormous capacity of machinery in the factory. This applied particularly to machinery that required large initial investments in capital (money). Here the key challenge for management was to develop new systems of organizational design and control.

Perhaps no individual is more closely associated with this transformation than Frederick Winslow Taylor, the man would come to be known as the father of scientific management. Taylor was born in 1856, at the outset of a great industrial expansion in the United States. This era ushered in the rise of industrial empires, particularly in iron and steel. It also witnessed the older and once dominant "owner as manager" model of industrial capitalism give way to professional managers who came to run the great corporations of the late nineteenth and twentieth centuries for their owners and stockholders. This was also an era of turmoil and unrest, particularly in Europe, where labor disputes were chronic, and where the fate of capitalism, which would become the dominant economic system over the twentieth century, was far from settled.

Taylor himself was born into a life of affluence and privilege; his father was a wealthy merchant. But Taylor rejected the sensibilities and values of his class upbringing, as well as its interest in a classical education that placed great emphasis on music, poetry, and the arts. Instead, he turned his interests toward practical pursuits, gaining valuable experience working as a machinist as a young man and later becoming an accomplished engineer.

While it seems that Taylor should have enjoyed privilege and material comforts during adulthood, his inner life was filled with turmoil, and he suffered from lifelong neurosis. His method for coping with these psychological struggles was to live an ascetic and highly driven life; he developed and lived by highly disciplined and meticulously prescribed routines. It is somewhat ironic, and perhaps an unsettling commentary about the values and principles that underlie our modern industrial order, that Taylor (and his lifestyle) represented the ideal character type for developing new methods of managing factory life, and later, all manner of business activity.

The genius of Taylor's vision for managing industrial enterprises was to promote a system that transferred the traditional working methods, practical knowledge, and modes of cooperation among workers, to management, thereby leaving workers with the simplified, but much more tightly controlled, responsibility of following directions and doing the requisite manual labor. Taylor envisioned his system as an answer to what was commonly referred to as the *labor problem*—the endless and oftentimes very open and heated conflicts between factory owners and managers on the one side, and their wage laborers on the other, with the ultimate struggle taking place over the control and direction of the very capitalist system itself. Taylor believed that his approach would promote increased productivity and, with it, *mutual prosperity*, to be shared among owners of capital, management, and labor for the benefit of all. His seminal work, *The Principles of Scientific Management*, was published in 1911 and caused a worldwide sensation; it was rapidly translated into almost a dozen languages.

Taylor's approach (which he referred to as "scientific management") involved a few simple principles, but the process through which this system was adapted was anything but smooth and simple. His ideas faced widespread resistance from workers and labor organizations, leading to serious questions throughout the wider society as to the moral–ethical acceptability of such a system of industrial management and even sparking a congressional investigation. But Taylor remained a tireless champion for his new methods. He firmly believed that scientific management, by greatly increasing productivity, could pave the way towards maximum prosperity for each of the antagonistic parties.

Scientific management involved a few key principles. First, management must gather the wellspring of traditional knowledge that had largely been under the control and purview of workers, and through careful experimentation, via time and motion studies, develop the most effective system for accomplishing any task. This literally involved using a stop watch to carefully record the duration of each simple motion that makes up a more complex series of tasks or a collective grouping of tasks. Next, workers had to be carefully selected and trained to carry out tasks as defined under the new system (as opposed to developing their own means and methods or continuing previous practices). Third, management must establish a system of supervision to ensure that the work was carried out in accordance with the scientific principles that had been established. Finally, an overarching division of responsibility between management and workers had to be firmly established in a way that ensured that management's exclusive responsibility was to control the development of methods and routines for the accomplishment of tasks and the overall organization of work, whereas workers responsibility was carrying out the physical labor itself. This resulted in a strict separation between mental and physical labor, or more simply put, between thinking and doing.

The spirit of scientific management was captured and widely acclaimed in the development of the moving assembly line introduced by Henry Ford in 1913. This simple organizational innovation (which was instrumental in the production of Ford's famous Model T) involved a giant conveyor belt that brought interchangeable parts to the workers, replacing the time-consuming and somewhat disorganized process whereby workers walked from one assembly station to the next, picking up needed parts and carrying them elsewhere. The evolution of Fordism spawned an industrial system of mass production of homogeneous (similar) products on a grand scale. It generally required high levels of capital investment (money) in manufacturing plant and equipment that was designed for fixed purposes and operated under the assembly line model. Of course, this entailed the standardization, regimentation, and simplification of work routines in the factory.

Nowhere was this Fordist production system, and the emerging industrial society over which this system was exerting a pervasive influence, better captured than in the biting social protest film *Modern Times*, created by legendary silent-film maker Charlie Chaplin. In this film, which is set during the economic devastation of the 1930s Great Depression era, Chaplin (starring in his renowned role as movie audiences' favorite tramp) finds employment on the assembly line at the fictitious Electro Steel Corp. As he performs his job of tightening bolts onto machine parts that flow endlessly along a moving assembly line, we come to see the dehumanizing features of the factory system in the machine age. The line moves quickly; to keep up, Charlie must endlessly reproduce a series of tightly controlled repetitive motions, being careful not to miss any of the parts that pass through his station and "feed" the big machines around which the factory's production system is organized.

After performing these highly controlled tasks for hours on end, with few breaks in between, Charlie develops tics and quirks—when he goes on a break, he cannot stop his arms and body from making the repetitive motions required of him on the production line. By the end of the workday, during which management has sped up the assembly line, Charlie has been literally been driven crazy by the work. The movie reaches a climax when Charlie, struggling to keep up with the accelerated workflow, flops himself onto the moving assembly line and compulsively strives to tighten every bolt he can get his wrench around. Caught up in the vast machinery, Charlie is fed through its cogs and wheels until the

Created by the great Charlie Chaplin, the 1936 Great Depression-era movie *Modern Times* is a satire on industrial society. Reprising his famous tramp role, Chaplin plays a factory worker who eventually gets swallowed up by the industrial machinery—a metaphor for the greater and widespread fear that the industrial society was swallowing up humanity. *(Photofest)*

line is reversed and the machine spits him back out. At that point Charlie takes flight; as his coworkers chase him around the factory floor attempting to subdue him, Charlie flutters about, still compulsively applying his wrench to anything that looks remotely like the bolts he has been tightening on the assembly line. In the end, he is taken away to a psychiatric ward—turning all of those nuts and bolts has truly made him nuts. The movie continues with Charlie embarking on many other hilarious adventures, each of which is a commentary on the absurdities of industrial society.

In the end, modern industrial times marched onward. In many respects, an implicit bargain was struck as multitudes of workers over subsequent generations consented to extensive managerial control of their working lives in exchange for the opportunity to enjoy the growing prosperity of a mass consumer society. As a testament to efficiency, Taylor's principles and Ford's production system eventually made it possible for the average factory worker to purchase an automobile for his family—and since the 1950s, even take them out for an affordable meal at a local fast-food restaurant.

McDONALDIZATION: FROM FACTORY TO FAST FOOD

As the twentieth century progressed, the rise of large-scale bureaucracies (in both government and business) became an omnipresent fact of life. Today, while bureaucracy is still seen everywhere, some sociologists posit that its once-rapid and inexorable advance has slowly ground to a halt. In connection with this, social theorist George Ritzer makes a compelling case that by the latter half of the twentieth century, a new prototype had emerged to transform our cultural landscape. This new organizational type embodied the core principles of rationalization and was therefore similar to bureaucracy in principle, but it had taken on a different form—the same form that defines a fast-food franchise. Ritzer encourages us to explore how the principles of rationalization and bureaucracy have become manifest in this new, more enticing, and marketable form. In fact, we can observe this form and its associated principles flowering all around us, through a process that Ritzer coined **McDonaldization**. In this new system, the principles underlying the systems and processes of the fast-food restaurant have come to characterize the way much of our world is organized today. But, new names and new theories can be deceiving—once we learn to look past the neon signs, the bright and colorful menus, and the shiny plastic surroundings, what remains is fundamentally the same old iron cage.

KEY ELEMENTS OF McDONALDIZATION

Ritzer's thesis about McDonaldization certainly brings to mind our earlier discussion of the great transformation to modernity. Accompanying this process were increasing levels of urbanization, industrialization, and democracy—and in connection with these, the notion of an increasing rationalization of society.

Sociologist George Ritzer argues that the underlying operating principles that define McDonald's have become a template adopted by many other facets of our social world. *(Wikipedia)*

As noted earlier in this volume, this idea of rationalization was first expounded by German sociologist Max Weber, who claimed that this process would eventually come to influence virtually all spheres of life and would also involve a

great change in the way people would come to understand and approach their world.

George Ritzer elaborates on this premise, pointing out that rationalization continues to advance and that the principles underlying the organization and operation of the fast-food industry are far more reflective of rationalization than of the older image of the bureaucracy, even though the core principles of each are very similar. In elevating the fast-food industry as a model for societal rationalization today, Ritzer identifies four key principles that shape the way the industry operates: efficiency, calculability, predictability, and control (primarily through technology). As we explore these principles, keep in mind that the fast-food industry is by no means the only place where rationalization informs our world today. On the contrary, this process permeates today's entire retail economy as well as other institutional domains, including the criminal justice system and other government functions, medicine and heath care, and the educational system.

Efficiency

The principles that undergird McDonaldization and McDonaldized systems are really variations on the themes that inform bureaucracy. First, and foremost, is the principle of **efficiency**, or the search for the most effective means for achieving some well defined end. Rationalization and McDonaldization are ultimately about creating systems, structures, and practices all aimed at the overarching goal of enhancing efficiency, which, under the capitalist system, leads to greater profitability. Imagine, for example, that you are the owner of a fast-food franchise. You have 12 employees that serve 300 hamburgers an hour to your hungry customers. Now, imagine reorganizing the way the work at your franchise is done so that you need only 8 employees to prepare and serve the same number of hamburgers. In implementing this reorganization, you save money on wages (8 employees are equivalent to two-thirds of your original 12).

This is just one example of how McDonaldization works in practice, but it illustrates a process that creates integrated and efficient systems. Another important way in which this is achieved is by narrowing and refining an organization's goals. This involves eliminating any unnecessary work involved in getting the requested product to the customer. Even more important to achieving efficiency is eliminating any aspects of the overall offerings provided for the customer that do not directly serve and enhance the achievement of that narrowly and precisely defined goal. In fact, this was the genius of the original McDonald brothers, Richard and Maurice, who founded McDonald's but later sold the business to Ray Kroc. After having run a successful drive-in restaurant in California during most of the 1940s, they transformed their operation along these very lines. Their innovations represent an achievement that has been heralded as a major advancement in rationalization of the entire fast-food industry.

How did they do it? The McDonald brothers eliminated, simplified, and standardized all aspects of their restaurant business operation. They eliminated carhop service, which had involved servers coming out to meet the customers parked in their automobiles, taking their orders, and then bringing their food to them. Instead they shifted operations toward a self-service counter. Then they simplified the menu, eliminating any items that could not be eaten with one's hands, thereby eliminating the need for utensils. They standardized and simplified burger preparation, making it easy for low-skilled "assemblers" at a few work stations to carry out the process and thus eliminating the need to employ (skilled) short-order cooks. Finally, they eliminated glassware and dishware, replacing them with disposable paper cups and wrapping. In the end, this system saved time and money and also made it feasible for working-class families to enjoy a dining out experience every so often.

Today, fast food and retail industries in general, are organized first and foremost around this overarching principle of efficiency. The process defines what they do and why they do it, as well as the overall experience of consumers. But what consumers see and experience is really only one part of a larger and more vastly organized system. This larger system is geared towards ensuring that the corporation develops, secures, and distributes product inventory to local franchises or establishments so that the same service/product can be provided for other customers in the same efficient and cost-effective manner.

Calculability

The overall mission and focus of any McDonaldized business or organization have to be narrowed and refined to encourage further rationalization and greater efficiency. This has led to the growing importance of the principle of **calculability**, which involves placing value or emphasis on quantification and quantifiable aspects of some product or service over the vaguer and more ambiguous principle of quality. This principle has inspired a marketing approach that has led to a wider cultural emphasis on such fast-food values as supersize, extra-value meals, and two-for-one, all of which indicate that more is better, or that quantity equals quality. Related values, such as those involving time as a commodity, are conveyed through the lure of 15-minute delivery, service in one hour, or 30-minute meals. Calculability is intimately tied to efficiency and provides an important yardstick by which today's consumer measures, understands, and values quality.

The fact that McDonaldized systems must utilize quantity over quality is built into the systems themselves. Recall how the innovations achieved by the McDonald brothers involved simplifying the menu and eliminating skilled short order cooks by replacing them with low-skilled food assemblers. Over time, McDonald's became a vast food empire that was able to get its food suppliers to deliver food products that met exact specifications (everything from flash frozen French fries, to frozen hamburger patties, to fish fillets and chicken nuggets). These in turn become the nuts and bolts of the highly organized and tightly controlled fast food assembly lines at thousands of franchises.

For the system to function effectively, hamburger patties have to be made to exact specifications, so that they can be placed in perfectly symmetrical grids on the grill and be cooked uniformly to the same level of doneness in the same amount of time. The burgers must also fit perfectly on prefabricated buns. Because of these and numerous other organizational constraints, McDonald's has imposed significant limitations on its ability to experiment with the quality of its hamburgers. However, the chain can offer you a ninety-nine cent McDouble or encourage you to supersize your meal for only seventy-five cents more, both examples of quantity as a substitute for quality, even though consumer outcry over the fast-food industry's contribution to obesity in children has led them to curb their enthusiasm for such options. Furthermore, the fast-food industry, as well as retail chains and franchises in general, have worked hard to encourage (dare we say "train"?) consumers to value the offerings that come off their assembly lines. One of the ways in which they do this is through the related principle of predictability.

Predictability

Students who have traveled abroad at some point in their college careers tell me that after being away for weeks or months, the familiar sight of a McDonald's golden arches or the green Starbuck's logo provides a comforting reminder of home. After navigating a foreign country, trying to learn the ropes, and oftentimes speak a new language, it sometimes feels good to relax in familiar surroundings and order food that offers a comforting sense of familiarity. That sense of familiarity and identification is not just something that we feel—it is something carefully cultivated and managed by corporations, especially restaurant chains. In fact, **predictability** is a core principle involved in the process of McDonaldization. The homogeneity of brands and signature offerings are intended to make us feel comfortable. We like knowing that the Big Mac or fries we eat in Chicago, will taste just the same as the ones we ate in New York, Paris, Rome, Moscow, or even Shanghai. Over the past century, corporations have taken great pains to nurture a preference for predictability among consumers, so that we now seek out and show preference for our favored franchises, wherever we may be.

Predictability has been an enormous boon to the corporate franchise system, and franchises that recognize this do everything possible to make this principle work for them. McDonald's, for instance has gone to great lengths to ensure that their fries and burgers taste virtually the same in any of their thousands of franchises worldwide. Predictability enables corporations to take advantage of large-scale production and distribution systems that serve their many franchises or retail chain outlets. To produce a uniform (and thus predictable) product, each franchise has to have the same equipment and the same raw (well, oftentimes it comes frozen) material inputs.

Ritzer also reminds us that this principle of predictability is in no way limited to fast food, and although McDonald's is credited with being the prototype for this process, we can also see the modern shopping mall as a monument to predictability. Inside any typical mall are dozens of retail chains that can be found at almost any other mall throughout the country, if not throughout the world. So, once again, you can travel from New York to Chicago, or from L.A. to D.C., and have virtually the same kind of mall shopping experiences in any one of these cities.

Once you start to look for it, McDonaldized predictability is everywhere. It can be observed in common rituals such as staying home on a Friday night to enjoy a TV dinner and a movie, or during the annual family vacation, which may involve a trip to an amusement park or perhaps an exotic beachfront location, and lodging at a hotel or campground. With respect to dinner and a movie, Ritzer notes how the advent of the TV dinner, which has been transformed into the microwave meal over recent decades, represented a major milestone in the evolution of a predictable and homogenous American cuisine. In major grocery chains throughout the United States, one has access to the same diverse range of predictable microwaveable meals. You can sit down to such a meal on a Friday night, enjoying an entrée inspired by one of a variety of cuisines, ranging from traditional home-style American, to Chinese, Italian, or Mexican. You

No matter where you travel, be it Boston to Barcelona or Sao Paulo to Paris, McDonald's fries will always taste the same. The principle of predictability has advanced far beyond burgers, fries, and fast food. It now engulfs virtually all aspects of retail and consumer experiences. *(Wikipedia)*

can combine this experience with a rented movie, perhaps a predictable sequel to a favorite original produced just a few years earlier. The explosion of movie sequels provides the opportunity for moviegoers to relive a pleasurable experience, with some modifications to familiar storylines and characters; this is predictable fare, which provides a stream of profit for the motion picture industry. Over the years, popular movies such as *Die Hard*, *Rocky*, *Batman*, *Superman*, *Star Wars*, *X-Men*, *Indiana Jones*, *Harry Potter*, *Toy Story*, *Legally Blond*, and *Revenge of the Nerds*, have all been followed up with sequels.

Many family vacation options have now become quite "packaged" and predictable as well. For those who can afford it, Beaches Resorts provides prepackaged, family vacations to its chain of Caribbean Island destinations. Each package comes complete with all inclusive meals, an array of water sports, and supervised activities for the kids. They even have Sesame Street stage shows for the little ones. But if roughing it with a bit of camping is more to your family's liking and budget, how about visiting one of Yogi Bear's Jellystone Park camp resorts, or "KOAs," a franchise network of campgrounds focused on providing family vacations throughout the United States. Here again we see predictability in the tent or RV camping sites or cabin rentals being offered. Furthermore each of the Jellystone franchise locations includes a recreational staff that promises to provide your family with an "unforgettable experience." How about starting the day with a flag raising featuring Yogi Bear? Then fill the rest of your day with arts and crafts, swimming and a movie. Bingo, karaoke, and live bands keep the adults entertained too.

By this point it has probably become clear that corporate chains and franchises have moved well beyond the realm of fast food in shaping the retail environment and that they have served to make many of our consumption experiences highly predictable and uniform in nature. But in the process they have also worked hard to inculcate in consumers the desire for the comforts that accompany the branded or franchised consumption experience. For example, food and retail chains go to great lengths, oftentimes spending a great deal of energy and money on marketing and advertising, in their efforts to encourage our attachments to their respective brands. As a child, I recall looking forward to being able to take my best friends to McDonald's for lunch on my birthday. My own son prefers Taco Bell. But, in the end, it's the same general process at work.

Control

A final principle of McDonaldization is **control**, which is achieved through *organizational practices* and *new technologies*. Much like the others, the principle of control deeply affects both workers and consumers, all of whom have come to accept a high degree of control when interfacing with McDonaldized systems, and especially fast-food franchises. Of course, the nature, depth, and duration of control is certainly greater for workers in such systems, particularly in the fast-food industry, than it is for customers. In either case, control is important for achieving efficiency and as well as ensuring predictability in any McDonaldized system.

Customers may be controlled in a variety of ways. First, as George Ritzer points out, fast-food restaurants are certainly anxious for you to stop by for a meal, but they are also keen on making sure that you do not stay too long, if at all. In fact, the drive-through window offers the ultimate level of organizational control and efficiency: Customers place their orders from their cars, without ever having to enter the restaurant. Then they simply drive away with their food as well as their garbage. You might well wonder why anyone would even enter a fast-food restaurant when a drive thru is available. I agree with you, and so would most people. Our culture places great importance on speed and convenience and we've become accustomed to this. In many respects, we truly live in a fast-food culture. And why indeed should we inconvenience ourselves by entering the fast-food restaurant, which almost invariably means dealing with uncomfortable seats and overly bright lights, having to get your own drinks, napkins, and condiments, and then bus your own table when the meal is finished.

Other forms of control are reflected in that fact that fast-food franchises tend to offer limited menus with prescribed offerings. At McDonald's and at other fast-food restaurants, we normally do not order a hamburger the old-fashioned way (with or without cheese, lettuce, tomato, ketchup, etc.). Instead, we use the names and scripts displayed for us on the restaurant's menu and ask for a Big Mac, a Whopper, a Homestyle Griller, or a Big N Tasty. This lingo makes for quick and efficient ordering—every stroke and every extra movement increases the cost of doing business, and because the selected items normally having their own dedicated key on the restaurant's cash register, it makes for efficient order processing.

Employees or workers in McDonaldized settings tend to have their actions scripted into a few simple movements or motions. If they interface with customers, they often have prepared scripts to recite. Even the drive-through services are likely to have a script: A prerecorded voice (technology) greets customers, usually encouraging them to try some new offering or add something to their orders. Once the initial greeting is initiated, a human server continues processing the order. As Robin Leidner notes in her book *Fast Food, Fast Talk*, however, this is an extension of the prescripted process that can be seen at all McDonald's counters. Window servers handle customer orders by following a six-step process as prescribed by corporate headquarters, which maintains an extensively detailed operations and training manual that is informally referred to as "the Bible."

The traditional work of order-taking servers have been progressively replaced by automated technologies that are far more predictable and program-

Fast-food and other retail corporations increasingly employ advanced elements of technological and organizational control in providing customer service. Whenever you visit a drive thru, it is increasingly likely that the first voice you hear will be an automated one. This is usually followed by human interaction with a server, in a "conversation" that is tightly scripted by the corporation. *(Shutterstock)*

mable than human beings. This is also the case with food preparers, who work with increasingly advanced and automated equipment that serves to eliminate much of the uncertainly and the errors made by human workers. Thus, much of the cooking and serving processes are now controlled and monitored by machine technology. McDonald's, for instance, does not leave it to the discretion and judgment of its workers to gauge when the griddle is at the right temperature, when the hamburgers are ready to be turned, when the fries are done, and even, how much soda is needed to fill up a cup. All these things are all extensively controlled by and calibrated into the kitchen equipment, leaving the humans only a limited number of key tasks to perform that support the work of the machines. If the word "Taylorism" comes to mind, you are on the right track.

Finally, although our examples of control have been focused explicitly on the fast food industry, we must take a moment to ponder how the principle of control has extended well beyond this one industry into the retail corporate service sector. Let's consider just one example: control through technology and automation. This is something we see in almost every transaction with telephone, Internet, and airline service providers (as well as countless others) that provide customer service and support call centers (operated in various parts of the globe) with computerized voice answering systems. These systems generally have prescribed menu options, with scripted question and answer protocols. They often have very long "hold" times. Once you finally get to talk to a real human being, it is very likely that he or she is also following a tightly controlled script.

Many of these customer service systems are becoming completely automated and all encompassing. They allow the customer to pay a bill, make an adjustment in services, or request technical support assistance, without ever having to leave the house or speak to another human being. In fact, if you ever do get to speak with a live human, it might even cost you a few dollars extra for the privilege. One aspect of this trend is the increasing use of computer-based online services, which mean that the best one can hope for is a live chat with service support personnel. In some cases, it is difficult to know whether you are dealing with a human being or a voice automated program. What we do know is that these systems continue to evolve in a way that draws the customer ever deeper into the orbit of growing rationalization—while eliminating or drastically reducing entire segments of the service industry workforce.

McDONALDIZATION AND CULTURE: CONSUMER-CITIZENS RESPOND

In this concluding section of the chapter we look briefly at the different ways people respond to the McDonaldization of the world around us. We will examine responses of individual consumers and responses of corporations that modify McDonaldization to suit their specific purposes. Finally, we will examine McDonaldization in the context of institutional life and raise questions about the way in which this process, like wider rationalization, affects our institutions. We will also identify some ways we may have an effect upon McDonaldization.

How Individual Consumers Respond to McDonaldization

In his investigation into the McDonaldization of society, George Ritzer asks what individuals can do to cope with an increasingly McDonaldized world. The answer, he notes, depends upon one's attitude toward McDonaldization. While reading this chapter, you may have thought to yourself that Taylorism and McDonaldization are really no big deal. They simply reflect the way in which our world is ordered, and there is not much to be done about it. Things are the way they are, and humans find ways to adapt. Ritzer, in fact, hypothesizes that individuals may adopt a range of responses to McDonaldization, from fully embracing it, to rejecting it outright, with many other responses falling somewhere in between these extremes. Furthermore, Ritzer links McDonaldization (rightly so) to Weber's image of the iron cage of rationalization.

Interestingly enough, Ritzer posits that for some people, living in a McDonaldized world is like living in a *velvet cage*. By this he means that some people are quite comfortable living in such a world. Such individuals embrace the uniformity and predictability that McDonald's and other fast-food chains (along with a host of corporate retail establishments) offer. They like the homogenized choices, and they feel comfortable entering environments that offer them, whether it be during a stop for a bite to eat at the drive thru, a quick trip to the local shopping center, or a visit to an indoor shopping mall. These represent the world to which many of us have been socialized, and we would feel somewhat lost without them. Furthermore, many people are quite comfortable interacting with customer service representatives at corporate chains—the scripted process, albeit impersonal, is usually friendly and nonthreatening.

Other individuals view McDonaldization as a type of iron cage, but one that is flexible and made of rubber and therefore not entirely cold and rigid. Individuals who embrace a *rubber cage* image of their world constantly make trade-offs between McDonaldized (rationalized) and non-McDonaldized (nonrationalized) interactions. They may in fact envision that McDonaldization allows them to enjoy other types of nonrationalized pursuits. For instance, they may enjoy spending time in nature, going hiking, enjoying time at the beach, or playing sports with friends at a local park, but they also find that stopping for fast food along the way affords them time to engage in such nonrationalized activities. In the same light, there are those who enjoy the benefits of a large grocery chain, which stocks a large assortment of international and organic foods, and provides a convenient shopping experience, which enables them to explore new avenues of home cooking on the weekends.

Finally, there are those people who are deeply troubled by the McDonaldization of society. These individuals share in Max Weber's pessimism about the iron cage of rationalization. They are apprehensive that the advance of rationalization will continue with no end in sight, and they do not take great comfort in the notion that there are choices—that is, one can simply decide which elements of rationalization to accept and which elements to reject. Instead, they are most likely to imagine that an earlier, less rationalized world (or perhaps some future derationalized one) would be much preferable to the current state of affairs. Such individuals might be most receptive to social movements or political programs aimed at transforming the current world order in ways that deemphasize consumerism, or which put environmentalism and a lighter footprint (in terms of resource use) at the forefront of society's priorities.

How Corporations Respond to Consumers

One factor we should keep in mind while we examine how McDonaldization affects our lives is the way corporations have adapted and refined their approach to consumers. McDonaldization represents a set of operating principles that define the missions, services, and delivery process of many corporations, but these corporations often adjust the content of their offerings in sophisticated ways to appeal to specific or targeted segments of consumers. In recent years, in fact, McDonaldization has become a more sophisticated and complex process. This phenomenon has led George Ritzer to ask whether we have reached a historical juncture where this process is now better characterized by the operating philosophy and principles of Starbucks rather than McDonald's. A related question he poses is whether we rename this evolving process Starbuckization.

Ritzer (rightly) sticks with the term McDonaldization. But a comparison between these two examples of McDonaldization—one being the traditional model and the other being a somewhat younger upstart that has "reinvented" the older model with advancements and increasingly sophisticated applications of this process—reveals a great deal about how McDonaldization has evolved and assumed different forms or (literally) flavors. In the final analysis, however, the Starbuck's phenomenon seems to reflect the same basic principles that define McDonaldization.

We may think of the early McDonald's as having targeted a mass American market of consumers. Perhaps we can even think of McDonald's as the classic example of the all-American fast-food chain over the last fifty years. Today however McDonaldization is being used in more refined ways to target certain *demographics* (or categories of people based upon such characteristics as age, income, region of the country, ethnicity, gender, etc.). One indicator of this appears to be how different chains appeal to different lifestyles, political philosophies, and levels of affluence, among consumers. A recent survey of social and demographic trends by the Pew Research Center (www.pewresearch.org) helps us understand how retail corporations are approaching and adjusting McDonaldization to suit their specific purposes.

Titled "McDonald's and Starbucks: 43% Yin, 35% Yang," the Pew study, which surveyed over 2,000 American adults in 2008, asked the question: "Just for fun: Would you prefer to live in a place with more McDonald's or more Starbucks?" McDonald's won by a respectable margin—43 percent to 35 percent, with the remaining 20 percent of respondents indicating no preference. But if we break down the responses along certain key demographic categories, some interesting patterns emerge. For instance, Starbucks clearly appeals to a higher income segment of the population, with those making $75,000 a year or more preferring to live in a place with more Starbucks (48 percent) than McDonald's (34 percent). Education (which is often related to income levels) also influenced responses. College graduates preferred Starbucks (47 percent vs. 32 percent for McDonald's); those with a high school degree or less preferred McDonald's (50 percent) to Starbucks (26 percent). Finally, the responses suggest that there may indeed be something to the phrase "latte-drinking liberal," as liberals prefer Starbucks by 46 percent (33 percent opting for McDonald's), while conservatives preferred McDonald's (50 percent) to Starbucks (28 percent).

Ritzer notes that visionary entrepreneur Howard Schultz, who took over and transformed Starbucks from a Seattle-based coffee house into a national sensation, did seem to have a special vision or purpose in mind for the Starbucks chain. During the latter part of the 20th century the coffee Americans drank was pretty bad. Schultz wanted to educate consumers to the merits of drinking freshly ground coffee, brewed one cup at time, using high quality Arabica beans. He wanted to offer customers an affordable luxury, in a setting reminiscent of a lifestyle associated with European coffee houses—an oasis that offered opportunities for casual encounters and conversation.

Sociologist George Ritzer has explored the idea that McDonaldization may be replaced by Starbuckization, a new development that seems to involve a more intensive and sophisticated marketing approach aimed at resonating with an overall consumer experience, lifestyle, and identity. Are you more Starbucks or McDonald's? *(Wikipedia)*

In many respects, Schultz succeeded in his mission. In other respects, success changed the underlying goals—with the vast expansion of Starbucks coffee houses, their special coffee is generally brewed in large vats today, not one cup at a time, and the quality of the beans has declined as the company has had to increase its inventory (and use new sources) to supply its franchises. Starbucks has also been moving away from its signature ceramic mugs, replacing them with signature paper cups. Furthermore, Schultz's efforts to create a new and inviting space for customers to experience coffee shops, has not panned out as expected: 80 percent of sales today are "to go," with many Starbucks now even offering convenient drive thru service.

Ritzer, in his McDonaldization vs. Starbuckization speculations, posited that the Starbucks' incursion on McDonaldization could be viewed as "theatrics." What he means is that what Starbucks offers is not really coffee but an experience accompanied by coffee. Within this experience, employees and customers act out the "illusion of an old-fashioned coffee house." This is a very important observation. It directs our attention to how many corporations today seek to draw us into their rationalized offerings, by offering us new and enticing experiences that enhance the products they have to offer.

McDonaldization and Institutions: A Final Note

Earlier in this book we discussed how institutions and culture are educative. They teach us about who we are, what we should desire, and what goals we should pursue, even as we oftentimes simply view institutions as means to our own ends. However, we also stressed that institutions have an impact upon those ends (or on our values). McDonaldization first and foremost informs the institution of economy, but it is also part of a larger process of rationalization that informs how all of our institutions have come to function to a greater or lesser extent. This includes even the family.

We must therefore consider how McDonaldization and rationalization will continue apace, and that these will be difficult to modify in significant ways, because advancements associated with these processes often are accompanied by claims that they serve our needs for efficient and cost-effective services, providing consumers with what they want. We do have some measure of choice as to whether or not to participate in McDonaldized systems, but that choice is growing increasingly limited and constrained and often requires extensive personal resources (such as time and especially money) or some form of organized or collective support if it is to meaningfully exercised. Such support is generally garnered either through the institutions of politics and government (through legislation) or through successful consumer movements that influence corporations to modify their practices. For instance, we can observe the effect of consumer movements in the increasing availability of organic foods and the widespread use of recyclable packaging. In the end, we must be mindful of how rationalization and McDonaldization shape us as well as our institutions in powerful ways.

LOOKING AHEAD

In the following chapter, we will continue to draw upon Weber's ideas regarding growing rationalization and bureaucracy in the modern world. With these principles in mind we begin our exploration of contemporary institutions, starting with two of the most highly rationalized, the economy and politics. In examining these two interrelated institutions, we will briefly explore their evolution, and then take up major features of each, along with the most pressing challenges they face. We then examine family (friendship), religion, education, and the mass media. Finally, we explore how the institutional context of 21st--century society must be understood within a global context, at both the individual and institutional level.

Further Reading

Bratton, John, David Denham, and Linda Deutschmann. *Capitalism and Classical Sociological Theory.* Toronto: University of Toronto Press, 2009.

Kivisto, Peter. *Key Ideas in Sociology.* 2nd ed. Thousand Oaks, Calif.: Pine Forge, 2004.

Kroc, Ray A. *Grinding it Out: The Making of McDonald's.* Chicago: Contemporary Books, 1977.

Leidner, Robin. *Fast Food, Fast Talk.* Berkeley: University of California Press, 1993.

Macionis, John J. *Society: The Basics.* 10th ed. Upper Saddle River, N.J.: Prentice Hall, 2009.

Ritzer, George. *The McDonaldization of Society*: Thousand Oaks, Calif.: Pine Forge/Sage, 1993.

————. *Enchanting a Disenchanted World: Revolutionizing the Means of Consumption.* Thousand Oaks, Calif.: Pine Forge/Sage, 2005.

Schlosser, Eric. *Fast Food Nation: The Dark Side of the All American Meal.* New York: Harper Perennial, 2002.

Weber, Karl. Ed. *Food Inc.: A Participant Guide: How Industrial Food is Making Us Sicker, Fatter, and Poorer—And What You Can Do About It.* New York: Perseus Books, 2009.

CHAPTER 4

THE INSTITUTIONAL CONTEXT I: ECONOMICS AND POLITICS

The U.S. is unique. And just as we have the world's most advanced economy, military, and technology, we also have its most advanced oligarchy. . . . Although lobbying and campaign contributions certainly play major roles in the American political system . . . the American financial industry gained political power by amassing a kind of cultural capital—a belief system. Once, perhaps, what was good for General Motors was good for the country. Over the past decade, the attitude took hold that what was good for Wall Street was good for the country. The banking-and-securities industry has become one of the top contributors to political campaigns, but at the peak of its influence, it did not have to buy favors. . . . Wall Street is a very seductive place, imbued with an air of power. Its executives truly believe that they control the levers that make the world go round. A civil servant from Washington invited into their conference rooms, even if just for a meeting, could be forgiven for falling under their sway. Throughout my time at the IMF, I was struck by the easy access of leading financiers to the highest U.S. government officials, and the interweaving of the two career tracks. (Simon Johnson)

"We can either have democracy in this country or we can have great wealth concentrated in the hands of a few, but we can't have both." (Justice Louis Brandeis)

The first quote above was by Simon Johnson, who was the chief economist at the International Monetary Fund (IMF), an international lending institution that has on numerous occasions provided emergency funds to help stabilize the financial systems of nations in the global economy. It was taken from his widely read article on the recent (2007–2008) U.S. financial crisis, which appeared in the May 2009 edition of *The Atlantic* magazine. The second now famous quote is from legendary Supreme Court Justice Louis D. Brandeis, who served on the court from 1916–1939.

What both of these quotes have in common, and what they ask us to consider, is the view that when great wealth and economic power become concentrated in the hands of a small group of people, the fate of a political system that calls itself democratic hangs in the balance. In fact, the term **oligarchy**, which is used in the first quote, refers to rule by the few. Compare this with democracy, which implies rule by the many. In this chapter, we explore the social institutions of economics and politics, and one major theme running throughout is the deep historical relationship and interconnections between both realms.

IT WAS ONCE CALLED POLITICAL ECONOMY

We often think about the economy as inhabiting a separate and distinct territory, cut off from the other realms we inhabit in our everyday lives. We witness parents going off to work in the economy every day, while most of us don't really get to see or understand clearly what it is that they do there. But we do know that it is important to hold a job or maintain a business, because so much of the rest of life depends upon the income that job or business generates. This income helps sustain the household and maintain a way of life. You probably hope that one day in the coming years, after your formal schooling has been completed, you will find a place in the economy. You will land a job and forge a career (or even start a business) in this thing called the economy. In fact, parents and relatives may urge you to pursue precisely those educational opportunities that offer the best chance of landing a well-paying job and a lucrative career (in the economy). In the meantime, courtesy of the media, you are probably reading or hearing published or televised speeches by business leaders and politicians exhorting our leaders to keep the government out of the economy so that business can operate efficiently.

This notion of the economy as a separate and distinct realm that permeates our lives did not really exist until the dawn of the twentieth century. In fact, the older term to describe what we now call "economy" was **political economy**. This term clearly tempers the notion that economic activity somehow inhabits its own world or exists in a vacuum. The term political economy, in fact, implies that the economy is part of the larger fabric of social life and also acknowledges its deep interrelations with other institutional domains, especially the realm of politics and government.

In the 1987 movie *Wall Street* infamous financier Gordon Gekko proclaimed "Greed is good." The rationale underlying the recent era of business deregulation has been based, in an important sense, on that very principle. The 2010 sequel to the original film, *Wall Street: Money Never Sleeps,* continues the storyline in much the same vein. *(Photofest)*

Simon Johnson's comments (in the quote that begins this chapter) on the recent financial crisis provide a dramatic illustration of the importance of viewing economics and politics through the lens of political economy. In the article in which the quote appeared and in his book *13 Bankers: The Wall Street Takeover and the Next Financial Meltdown* (co-authored with James Kwak), Johnson points out how since the 1980s the financial sector (i.e., Wall Street, investors, traders, etc.) has vastly expanded in comparison to other parts of our economy, both in terms of the amount of economic activity that transpires in this sector as well as in terms of profits generated. Over time, this growth has led to increasing influence over the rest of the economy and over our political life. Johnson speaks of a Washington (politics)–Wall Street (finance) corridor of influence and activity, in which many leading Wall Street bankers have also had careers as government regulators and advisors and vice versa. Not surprisingly, this corridor of influence has had an great impact on today's economy—one obvious result is that the rules put in place as a result of the great stock market crash of 1929 and the Great Depression of the 1930s have been slowly dismantled. The past few decades have been an era of *deregulation*, with government permitting Wall Street bankers and investors greater freedom to carry out their activities with fewer controls and limits.

Wall Street investors took advantage of greater deregulation by developing ever more complex deals, the most significant of which involved buying up bundles of home mortgages (literally thousands at a time), which had traditionally been held by bankers in local communities across the United States, and reselling them to other investors. This process got so out of hand, that in the end, it seemed that the entire financial sector had placed a huge bet on one hope—that the housing market would continue to rise to ever greater heights. But why take such a gamble? And why did it create such an economic disaster? Because these investors had begun to purchase bundles of home mortgages, which realistically, the owners would never be able to pay off. In so doing, these investors put the entire U.S. financial system at risk, in essence treating it like a grand casino, and you know what happened next. The government had to step in and bail out the Wall Street banks in order to prevent another great depression. Notwithstanding the bail-outs and assurances that all will be well, we have been handed the most serious economic recession since the great depression. Everyday citizens have been left with a bleak job market and high unemployment that is likely to last for years to come, along with frighteningly high rates of foreclosures, because many families can no longer afford to make their home mortgage payments and lose their homes. And during this period of deep economic crisis, the Wall Street bankers have insisted on maintaining their lavish pay and bonuses, a wish that has perhaps been granted by the continuing existence of the Wall-Street–Washington corridor.

THE GREAT TRANSFORMATION TO CAPITALISM AND DEMOCRACY: A BRIEF REVIEW

Now that we have pointed out the importance of political economy for understanding the two institutions of economics and politics, we must also make brief mention of the great transformation to modernity that has shaped the evolution of these institutions in today's world. In Chapter 2 we explored how the process of *industrialization* transformed the nature of productive activity in dramatic ways. The Industrial Revolution involved a shift from small-scale home-based craft production to work in factories that housed expensive but very productive machinery. As the factory system assumed an ever greater presence in society, cities grew. This process of *urbanization* brought large numbers of people—both migrants from the countryside as well as immigrants from other countries— who had been accustomed to an agrarian way of life into newly crowded cities. As industrialization advanced, many urban centers grew haphazardly, with no overall plan and certainly without the benefit of basic public services.

Also recall how at the outset of the great transformation to modernity the American and French Revolutions of the late eighteenth century (1700s), sparked the birth of democratic forms of government, and that during the first half of the nineteenth century, many in Europe considered *democracy* a radical and threatening idea. Democracy was accompanied by a dramatic decline in the power and privileges once held by absolute monarchs and the old feudal-aristocratic order; it gave rise to a newly empowered bourgeoisie, consisting of small entrepreneurs (business owners) and property-owning landlords. As democratic systems of government assumed their place in society, industrial capitalism emerged as the predominant economic system. Soon after, social movements aimed at the enfranchisement of wage laborers developed. These groups also wanted the state (government) to respond to their needs and to serve their interests providing security and material comfort in this new order. Movements promoting racial and gender equality also emerged to expand the circle of democratic enfranchisement. It is within this context that we will explore the nature and evolution of the institutions of economics and politics.

THE INSTITUTION OF ECONOMY

In Chapter 1 we explained that *institutions* are major arenas of social life, which have distinctive goals, ends, or purposes (however imperfectly defined); which consist of related clusters of normative expectations; and which contain a distinctive set of interrelated statuses. The institution of economy organizes the production, distribution and consumption of goods and services. We normally assign statuses to people associated with these functions: employee, manager, investor, owner, etc.

In the United States and most of the world today, capitalism is the predominant economic system. This system is based on private ownership of property, and the ability of individuals to trade their property freely in a competitive system that emphasizes consumer choice. We often contrast capitalism with **socialism**, which is a system in which property and the means to carry out productive activity are collectively owned. In such a system the goals and purpose of productive activity are centrally planned or defined by the central government.

The capitalist system is really global in scope, with much economic activity crossing national borders. To an important degree, different countries or regions have come to specialize in economic activity focused on one or more sectors of the economy. The **primary sector** of the economy involves activities aimed at raw material and resource extraction (and perhaps cultivation) from the natural environment. If we look around the globe, those workers in countries that have limited economic and technological development, and the lowest overall incomes, are much more likely to be engaged in such primary-sector activities as farming, fishing, and mining, than are workers in more economically developed nations. The **secondary sector** of the economy is the one in which manufacturing takes place, where raw materials are transformed into finished goods. Here all sorts of goods are produced—from automobiles to refrigerators, from clothing and furniture to computers. Finally, the largest portion of employment in the global economy is found in the **tertiary sector**, often referred to as the service sector. In recent decades, some individuals and groups in the United States have raised concerns about the shift in overall employment from manufacturing (secondary sector) to services (tertiary sector). The question here is whether the service sector can supply the kinds of middle class jobs that were so enjoyed by growing numbers of American workers during the post-World War II era, the heyday of manufacturing in this country. Today over 70 percent of U.S. workers are employed in service activities of some type. These include a wide range of occupations and professions that include people that work in secretarial and administrative jobs; nurses, doctors, and home health care aides; restaurant workers; lawyers; advertising agents; and teachers.

The Free Market

As Robert Bellah and his associates point out in their book *The Good Society*, perhaps the most powerful and compelling image that America holds of itself and its economy harkens back to the late eighteenth and early nineteenth centuries. In fact, it is no mere coincidence that that the nation's celebrated year of independence (1776) was also the year in which Scottish political economist Adam Smith published *The Wealth of Nations,* arguably the most important and influential work on the promise and virtues of the capitalist system. In his book, Smith asserted that social prosperity would be served to the greatest extent if individuals were allowed to freely pursue their self-interests in the marketplace. According to Smith, increased trade and growing specialization in industry, along with free and open competition, would lead society to greater levels of social prosperity as if it were guided by an "invisible hand."

In the American context, a sympathetic vision for the nation's political economy was greatly inspired such figures as philosopher John Locke and founding father Thomas Jefferson. Bellah and colleagues (1991) emphasize how our time-honored beliefs in life, liberty, and the pursuit of happiness came to define the nature of our cherished freedom in highly individualistic terms. These were translated into the individual rights of property, which meant the freedom to buy, sell, and dispose of one's private property in competitive pursuit of wealth as one sees fit, without interference from the state. In this context, the state (or government) is presumed to exist to protect the individual right of property, the highest form of good. These principles expressed a kind of faith that such conditions would lead to the greatest degree of progress and human advancement, unleashing the creative and innovative spirit of the American people.

In essence, this earlier vision for the free market resonates with some of our deepest American cultural traditions about the meaning of freedom itself. This abiding American idealized self-image is one of an independent citizenry—and an image perhaps best captured by the English yeoman farmer, who was independent, of middling condition, hard working, honest, and industrious. Within this ideal construct individuals confronted one another more or less as economic and political equals. Perhaps this vision resonates with the fact that we celebrate the self-made entrepreneur (if not the farmer) today, especially one who emerges from humble beginnings and rises to success through honest and hard work bolstered by creative inspiration. And yet, the world out of which these late eighteenth and early nineteenth century thinkers emerged was dramatically transformed over subsequent generations as economic activity expanded in scale and scope, evolving from regional to national and then to international proportions. Furthermore, as early as the late nineteenth century, it became clear that the small-scale entrepreneur was going to have to compete with a much more formidable adversary on the economic horizon: the corporation.

Rise of the Corporation

The economy unfolded during the nineteenth century in ways that were not in keeping with the American self-image and the ideal of a free market consisting of small, independent, and relatively equal (politically and economically) producers. Instead, the fears of the founding fathers and of keen social observers (like Frenchman Alexis de Tocqueville) about great inequalities in wealth and power were slowly actualizing through the emergence of large scale industrial concerns. The problem was that this earlier, cherished vision of American democracy and economic freedom required some measure of political and

The late nineteenth century Gilded Age witnessed growing concerns over concentrated economic and political power among wealthy industrialists and private corporations, even as these facilitated major growth and expansion of the U.S. economy. A political cartoon of the time depicted John D. Rockefeller's Standard Oil Company as an octopus with its tentacles wrapped around other industries. *(Library of Congress)*

economic equality among citizens. An absence of this equality could mean the emergence of a kind of new economic royalty—a feudal aristocracy that granted itself a host special privileges while consigning the rest of the population to an inferior status.

By the late nineteenth century, in what has come to be known as the *gilded age*, vast business concerns emerged to dominate many sectors of the economy. Many, almost mythical, *captains of industry* emerged during this era. Among these were Andrew Carnegie, John D. Rockefeller, and Cornelius Vanderbilt, men who built their empires in steel, oil, and railroads, respectively. And the businesses they built exercised vast power and influence on the economy.

Accompanying this growth in big business was the growing dominance of the large *corporation*. Earlier in our nation's history, corporations were chartered by individual states to perform specific functions deemed to be in the public interest. Examples of such public interest endeavors included the chartering of churches, colleges, and companies formed to build roads or canals. These public interest corporations were granted special monopoly status with the reciprocal commitment that they serve only a specific, predefined public purpose. This practice eventually gave way to many state legislatures permitting corporations to form for *any* business purpose—after paying requisite fees for the privilege of doing so. Eventually, American courts came to treat the business corporation more or less as they would any other type of private economic actor (i.e., individual citizen). These corporate citizens could then enter into market-based contracts as if they were individual entrepreneurs, thus enjoying a minimum of state interference. Over time, they could also use their vast financial resources to influence the political process.

Unions as a Countervailing Power

As big business came to dominate increasing sectors of the economy, many individual workers struggled to organize collectively to gain some leverage in the negotiation process and achieve some influence over wages and working conditions. In fact, we can think of labor unions as growing up alongside of big business as an almost natural response to vulnerability and unequal standing that individual workers experienced in negotiating with large and powerful employers. The late great 20th century economist and statesman, John Kenneth Galbraith, referred to the rise of organized labor as a *countervailing power* to that wielded by big business and large corporations.

Today, it is very difficult for many Americans to understand the deeper role that unions played in our nation's history. One reason for this is that well under ten percent of private-sector workers in the United States belong to unions—an all-time low over the past half a century or more. Today, in fact, it is almost too easy to take for granted the rights and privileges that unions of the past worked so hard to secure. These include provisions such as the forty-hour work week, paid vacations, sick leave, overtime pay, pensions, workplace health and safety regulations, as well as raises commensurate with increases to the cost of living. Some of these provisions were formally institutionalized into the employment relationship; others were simply incorporated into widespread expectations held by workers and their employers and legitimized by practice over time. Ironically, many workers today can no longer take for granted several of these provisions.

Aside from securing a range of benefits and provisions related to employment contracts, there is another important role that unions have held as part of a countervailing power—offering their members (and in turn members of the broader society) an alternative version of ongoing events in the nation's economy and an alternative vision for the future. Over recent decades, however, this countervailing voice has been more muted. Union influence and membership peaked during the decades after World War II, but began to decline during the late 1970s and early 1980s. This trend has continued, and one cannot help wonder whether the muting of this once powerful countervailing force

Alan Hughes, Arkansas AFL-CIO president, leads a rally. Historically the most prominent formal association of labor unions in the United States has been the American Federation of Labor (AFL). Organized in 1886, the AFL merged with the Congress of Industrial Organization (CIO) during the 1950s to become the AFL-CIO. In 2005, two of the nation's most powerful unions, the Service Employees International Union and the International Brotherhood of Teamsters, resigned from the AFL-CIO to form the Change to Win Federation (CtW), whose aim is to reverse a long-term decline in union influence. More recently, the AFL-CIO and the CtW have made strides towards greater collaboration and a shared agenda. *(AP Photo/Danny Johnston)*

has played a part in some of the events that have recently shaken U.S. and world economies.

For instance, in one of the quotes presented at the beginning of this chapter, economist Simon Johnson pointed out the increased role of the financial sector in the economy since the early 1980s and how this paralleled a movement toward growing deregulation of the rules governing that very sector of the economy. You are probably too young to remember this, but prior to the walloping financial crisis of 2007–2008, we had the Savings and Loan crisis of the 1980s; the dramatic collapse and failure of hedge funds (entities that the *Financial Times* has described as the equivalent of Wall Street banks on speed) proffered by the firm Long Term Capital Management, the millennial bursting of the high-tech bubble that brought a rapid and dramatic decline in the stock market and shock to the economic system; and lastly the major accounting scandals that led to the collapse of high-profile firms like Enron and WorldCom.

What all of these crises had in common was some measure of bending, stretching, creative interpretation, or downright unlawful breaking of the increasingly lax rules governing the financial sector of the economy. And all of this was occurring in an economic landscape in which the once loud (and sometimes raucous) voice of organized labor had grown very quiet—just when a robust and influential countervailing power was most needed. Such a countervailing presence might have led to hard questions and might have focused the attention of the mass media, citizens, and politicians on visions and practices that were swirling unchallenged throughout the economic sphere. And that same countervailing power might have pointed out alternative approaches and perspectives on how the country should face the future.

20th Century Capitalism: From Uncertainty to Steady Work and Back Again

In his book *The Disposable American*, economic journalist Louis Uchitelle charts the rise and decline of employment security for the American worker over the past century. As we noted earlier in this chapter, during the late nineteenth century large industrial enterprises emerged on the American economic scene. Many of these, such as Andrew Carnegie's steel manufacturing concern, were overseen by the owners themselves. If the businesses were large enough, owners often turned to foremen who would handle the daily operations of their firms. These foremen generally exercised absolute power and control over a firm's labor force. They made hiring decisions, negotiated wages, and fired or let workers go, sometimes on the spot, depending on their own particular whims or personal relationships with workers. If a foreman hired you one day and did not care for your attitude or the quality of work, you could readily be told not to come back the next day. All in all, this type of employment environment created great uncertainty for workers, who had little security regarding their economic fates. In addition, what was once a nation of local economies was becoming unified into larger markets that were prone to economic booms and busts, with the latter leading to periods of widespread unemployment.

Over time, as industrial concerns began to grow in size and complexity, and as firms merged into partnerships or pooled their investments with others into joint stock corporations, the original owners often found themselves in need of professional managers to run their operations. Some early examples of this trend can be found in the great railroad corporations, such as the New York Central or the Pennsylvania Railroad. They were central to the formation of a national unified market economy that was made possible by the completion of the transcontinental railroad in 1869, which connected the Atlantic and Pacific coasts of the United States. These companies grew far too vast and complex for their original owners to manage, so they turned to professional managers and staff to oversee and run all aspects of their operations.

And with the rise of a more or less permanent rank of professional managers to run these huge operations came the makings of what became known as *welfare capitalism*. During the early twentieth century, some corporations had come to see the value in having more permanent long-term staff, as it took time to master complex organizational systems and operating procedures. Experience came to be increasingly valued and rewarded, and with this came loyalty and commitment on both sides of the employment relationship. One indicator of this growing compact was the rise of employee pensions and profit-sharing schemes. By 1916, over fifty percent of railroad employees had company provided retirement pensions. This system was never universal; at best it provided only fragmented coverage for the American workforce. However, it persisted and eventually came to reflect an important, albeit an increasingly distorted and unrealistic, image of how workers achieve security even in today's economy, especially with respect to regular pay increases, sick leave, vacation, and retirement benefits. This system of welfare capitalism continued to expand up until the Great Depression of the 1930s, when government was called upon to play a greater role in ensuring economic security for workers and their families. It must be noted that the efforts of organized workers' movements were also instrumental for institutionalizing this system of economic security over time.

With this system as a backdrop, the nation's economy evolved in such a way that by the 1950s job security and permanent employment (which implied annual raises, paid vacation, overtime pay, health insurance, pension plan, etc.) were becoming unquestioned elements of corporate employment. This system, furthermore, had a wider impact upon employers outside of the world of affluent corporations, because it prompted them to provide similar elements of security and permanence to the extent they could afford them. In this context, layoffs were widely understood to be a temporary interruption in steady employment.

The United States experienced several economic shocks during the 1970s, not the least of which was an oil crisis that led to substantial price inflation that had an impact on the entire economy. The country also had to face a new concern—serious competition in the manufacturing sector from foreign corporations based in Europe and, especially, Japan. And so, while some management experts were calling for new styles of managing to meet the needs of an increasingly sophisticated and educated workforce, there was a crisis of business confidence that created an impetus to institute new organizational approaches to motivating workers and encouraging greater commitment and productivity. It should also be mentioned that corporations were increasingly eager to rewrite the employment contract, hoping to reduce the power and influence of unions in the workplace.

As part of this new crisis mentality, business leaders and their political allies were very successful in convincing the American public that the United States had entered a new and competitive economic environment in which not only survival but ever increasing corporate profitability must become the ultimate standard by which to judge management decisions. This came to mean that corporations must please Wall Street and global investors first and foremost, and do so within ever shorter time horizons. Thus, as Uchitelle concludes, we have come to witness widespread acceptance throughout American society of corporate layoffs, even if such layoffs occur only to increase profits; the focus on "saving the ship" has shifted to all manner of less than permanent and secure employment arrangements.

New Ways of Organizing: Teams and Knowledge Workers

As noted above, feeding into the crisis of confidence in American business that emerged during the late 1970s were management experts who were calling for new styles of managing and new organizational approaches to meet the needs of an increasingly sophisticated and educated workforce, with the complementary goal of ensuring greater commitment and productivity to help businesses survive in a more competitive environment. Throughout the 1980s and 1990s, American business leaders became enamored of the management and organizational practices found among Japanese auto manufacturers, whose reputations had been transformed from makers of cheap and unreliable products to the standard bearers of quality and excellence in manufacturing over the course of the late twentieth century. As James P. Womack and his co-authors explained in their book *The Machine that Changed the World,* Japanese auto manufacturers had developed a system which came to be known as *lean production.* This system supposedly took the best of craft production (with its emphasis on quality and highly skilled work) and mass production (which affords high volumes of production and therefore lower production costs) and blended them into a new way of manufacturing. The hope was that it would help to promote greater communication and cooperation among workers, overcoming some of the rigidity that typically defines bureaucratic organizations.

Researcher Laurie Graham went undercover as a factory worker in a Japanese automobile transplant in the Midwest, with the mission of exploring how the Japanese management model transferred to an American context. She wanted to see firsthand whether many of the claims made about the Japanese management style were true. Her experience and her findings and conclusions are described in her book *On the Line at Subaru-Isuzu*.

Proponents of the lean production model argue that workers experience greater levels of control and responsibility in the workplace, which elicits greater commitment and loyalty from them towards to organization. In the end, they posit, this system generates the dual benefits of increased employee satisfaction and greater productivity for management. Some critics of this model argue that it serves to undermine unions and actually reduces workers' sense of control.

What Graham experienced was a strong company culture that focused on teamwork, high levels of worker commitment, and an emphasis on continuous improvement. This focus on continuous improvement in the workplace is captured by the Japanese term *kaizen*, which translates loosely into "always searching for a better way." What she also experienced as a factory worker was the demand to rapidly carry out a high number of coordinated and repetitive motions endlessly throughout the course of the workday. In connection with this, she also noted that many workers developed repetitive motion injuries, especially to their hands and wrists, as a result of working in the factory. Furthermore, she noted somewhat ironically that while workers were more closely monitored and supervised than proponents of the model might suggest, they were encouraged to develop innovations around how the work of these highly productive teams should be carried out. This entailed having workers regularly conduct time and motion studies on one another. In effect, they were actually trained to "Taylorize" themselves—that is, to use and conform to the scientific management model described in Chapter 3 of this book.

Related to this new management focus is another term denoting a relatively new job description: *knowledge worker*. Such workers are much in demand in today's economy. They are highly skilled, knowledgeable, creative, and able to work in a cooperative team environment. They are good at mutual problem solving and often required to engage in continuous learning on and off the job. As technology continues to get more sophisticated, and computerized machines handle more of the routine tasks associated with manufacturing as well as service work, humans must be able to handle higher level responsibilities. The task of knowledge workers then is to utilize the capabilities and potential of computerized systems to solve problems, develop creative ideas, and serve customer needs.

The knowledge worker, who is part of a highly productive team, has become an icon of sorts in the modern economy, especially in the advanced or high-tech sectors. However, this ideal worker does not seem to reflect the kinds of skills and capabilities required of workers in the sectors of the economy that have been experiencing the highest levels of job growth in recent years. Instead, this job growth is most evident in low-wage service jobs in the retail, restaurant, and health care sectors of the economy. In fact, over the past few decades, it is giant mass merchandise retailer Wal-Mart that has become emblematic of major employment trends in the U.S. economy. What this trend in job growth means is that the "knowledge worker" positions supposedly valued by U.S. corporations are not being created to the extent anticipated. Moreover, the retail and food service sectors of the economy are notorious for creating jobs that are almost overwhelmingly part-time positions with low pay and few or no benefits (health care, sick leave, vacation, and retirement plans may or may not be included in the terms of employment). Clearly a major economic challenge we face in the twenty-first century is how to shift the balance in employment from low-wage service work to knowledge work, a shift that would improve the economic environment for workers and businesses alike.

THE INSTITUTION OF POLITICS AND GOVERNMENT

Having introduced the political economy perspective and provided an in-depth exploration of the institution of the economy, we now turn to the related institution of politics and government. As explained in Chapter 1, politics is a social institution that defines values, sets priorities, and establishes goals, all with the aim of mobilizing resources for achieving the collective ends or purposes of a society. Government is the organized means through which politics are carried out or administered. The manner in which the relationship between government and the economy is defined, and the roles and responsibilities assumed by each for advancing freedom, material well-being, and social welfare, have dramatic consequences for the nature of society itself. In the sections that follow we will explore the nature of modern democracy by briefly comparing it with other major forms of government. We will then explore the evolution of government in the United States over the past century or so, and finish by pointing out a few key challenges facing the country today.

Modern Democracy and Rational-Legal Authority

Chapter 2 and the brief overview presented at the beginning of this chapter described a key development in the transition to modernity—the rise of democratic systems of government. A democracy is a political system that grants power to the people as a whole. Core principles that inform democracy are those of individual freedom and equality, as well as a voice for all people in directing the nation's affairs. Also recall sociologist Max Weber's interest in democrati-

President Barack Obama speaks to a joint session of Congress. Because direct political participation in the daily affairs of governing our country is impractical, we exercise indirect participation through our elected representatives who legislate on our behalf. *(Wikipedia)*

zation as part of an overall rationalization process. Weber believed that direct political participation among the citizenry would become increasingly impractical with the growth of large nation states. At the same time he envisioned indirect participation through *representative forms of democracy* in which elected officials are granted wide decision-making authority by the populace.

Weber's interest in various forms of political **authority**, wherein people view the exercise of power by those who rule as legitimate, is helpful to us in understanding the basic foundation upon which democracy rests. He contrasted this type of authority with forms that were more typically found in earlier times. One such form was traditional authority, and it was this form that characterized political rule in Europe under the feudal system, which eventually gave way to capitalism. In this earlier context, traditional authority literally meant that the sanctity of tradition defined who could legitimately rule a territory, and also in this context, rule was assumed by monarchs and nobles, with authority passing down through male heirs of the ruling aristocracy.

The monarchic system of government, in which a single family rules from one generation to the next, was most commonly found in agrarian societies. To the extent that monarchies have persisted into the present age, they have generally been transformed into **constitutional monarchies** in which the monarch is nominal head of state with powers delimited by a constitution. Other systems of government on the world scene today rely more on raw power than legitimacy to function and are classified as **authoritarianism**, a system of government that basically denies people formal rights. In a similar vein, **totalitarianism** is a system that not only denies people rights but also extensively controls their lives. In terms of his overall schema, Weber was less interested in these last two forms of government because they lacked the potential for any basis in legitimacy. This is not to say that he denied their existence. To the contrary, Weber was keenly sensitive to the role of power in shaping human affairs.

Traditional authority involved a somewhat haphazard and informal system of administration, with monarchs granting authority to trusted and loyal advisors. In contrast, the emergence of rational-legal authority under modernity and democracy witnessed the rise of a far more rational and efficient system of administration. Under a system of **rational-legal authority**, elected officials owe their obedience to what is commonly referred to as the rule of law. This means that formally enacted legal rules define the nature of the electoral process, and the nature and degree of decision-making authority granted to elected officials. In the end, officials maintain the consent of the governed by operating within the legally defined boundaries that circumscribe their positions.

Weber noted that modern forms of governing required large administrative staffs having a wide range of formally trained technical experts who are given a good measure of latitude to carry out their duties. Loyalty in this context is, in principle, not to be given to the elected official (or to the monarch, as would have been expected under traditional authority), but is instead accorded to the legally defined parameters of the administrative position. The administrative apparatus under rational-legal authority, according to Weber, achieved powers, capabilities, and a degree of efficiency unparalleled in earlier times. However, this powerful administrative apparatus was not without cost to the overall democratic process, as the knowledge, experience, and discretion, assumed by technical experts, served to remove many aspects of the process of governing from the immediate understandings of everyday citizens. Bureaucracy, the organizational model through which rational-legal authority came to be exercised, was viewed by Weber as the ultimate manifestation of the rationalization process.

In *Key Ideas in Sociology,* Peter Kivisto points out that many social observers have defined the past two centuries as the democratic age. He notes how two major events marked this age at either end. The first was the fall of the Bastille in 1789 (just over a decade after the American Revolution), when the French people destroyed an infamous prison that represented the oppressive rule of the French monarchy and signaled the beginning of the French Revolution. The final event, according to Kivisto, was the fall of the Berlin Wall in 1989, which marked the end of the totalitarian and communist regime of the former Soviet Union and simultaneously marked the triumph of democracy and capitalism as the virtually uncontested models of political and economic systems throughout the world. Within that larger historical backdrop there have been many smaller, but very significant, changes in the nature of democratic society itself, especially with respect to the economy. In the next section, we examine similar important shifts that have taken place in U.S. government and politics over the past century.

The 20th Century State: From Laissez-Faire to Keynesianism and Back Again

During the nineteenth century, American corporations were chartered to perform specific functions deemed to serve the public interest, but the dominant political philosophy of the time was **laissez-faire**, a French term that literally means to leave or let alone and has come to mean a condition in which government plays a minimal role in the affairs of the economy. This philosophy fit with the nation's early self-image as conveyed by interpretations of Locke and Jefferson (discussed earlier) and eventually supported the vast business concerns created in the late 19th century by the captains of industry of the *Gilded Age* (Carnegie, Rockefeller, Vanderbilt, and others).

The Gilded Age gave way to what came to be known as the *Progressive Era*, a time during the late nineteenth and early twentieth century in which there was great concern about the growing presence and power of large businesses corporations in America. There was special concern raised over the influence of *monopolies*, where one company completely dominates a specific market by eliminating any competition then setting pricing and terms to serve its own narrow interests at the expense of consumers. Related to this was the rise of business *trusts*, where a group of firms would take control of some specific segment of the market. Social movements emerged in response to a wide range of concerns, which included business concentrations but also the widespread effects of industrialization (urban poverty and the need for education, safe workplaces, proper sanitation, etc.). These culminated in the election of Theodore Roosevelt as President in 1901. Roosevelt believed that big business could serve the general interest and welfare but was also committed to the idea that government must regulate its activities to ensure that this occurs.

The Progressive Era waned by the end of the first World War, ushering in the *Roaring Twenties* and setting the stage for the great stock market collapse of 1929 and the subsequent Great Depression of the 1930s, an era marked by massive business failures and skyrocketing unemployment. Viewed through the prism of events that led up to and came directly after the Great Depression, the Progressive Era seemed to temper some of the harsher features of laissez-faire capitalism but certainly did not lead to any fundamental reevaluation of this system. Historian Richard Parker, in his biography of the late economist and statesman John Kenneth Galbraith, conveys how the young Galbraith (then a young graduate student at Harvard University) was distressed by the reaction of his economics professors to the Great Depression. Many of these professors were highly respected figures, and their status as knowledgeable and reputable economists placed them in positions to offer advice and counsel to the country's political leaders. Most of them, however, advocated taking no action to halt the economic devastation of the Great Depression, believing that the economy operated under its own laws of development and any action taken by any government to interfere with this process would do nothing but create further harm.

The New Deal and Keynesianism Triumph over Laissez-Faire

Of course, such a passive laissez-faire approach to governing was unacceptable throughout the presidency of Franklin D. Roosevelt, who responded to the Great Depression with policies and legislation that came to characterize the *New Deal* era. These policies included such measures as the creation of the Works Project Administration (WPA), which by the late 1930s was employing more than a million workers in infrastructure projects. These workers built roads, dams, bridges, and buildings that would eventually support the flow of commerce and economic activity. This approach to government taking a role in generating economic development and prosperity has come to be known as **Keynesianism.** Named after John Maynard Keynes, a famous British economist of the era, Keynesianism is based on a simple principle—that government should step in and take the role of employer of last resort when business demand is slow or slack, so that workers have steady employment. In addition, government should carry out this mission by taking on useful projects that will help spur further economic activity and make the economy more productive in general, but which individual business are less likely to initiate themselves.

As another element of the New Deal during the 1930s, the federal government produced legislation to support efforts of workers to organize, bargain collectively, form unions, and have the legal right to strike. It was from this federal intervention that minimum wage laws were enacted and the 40-hour work week was established. The New Deal also witnessed the creation of the Social Security Act, which was established to provide pensions to retired workers in their old age.

The effects of the Great Depression lingered until the United States entered World War II. In Keynesian terms, the war turned out to be a massive economic development and jobs program for the county. Factories had to be converted to accommodate war-time production and run at full capacity to produce armaments, tanks, ships, and airplanes, among other things. World War II, in fact, set the stage for a novelty in the American workforce—the iconic Rosie the Riveter, who came to symbolize the great number of women employed in the factories that made up the war industries. Many of these women, it should be noted, were forced to leave the factories after the war to make room for return-ing male soldiers—neither the Great Depression nor World War II had changed social attitudes about discrete gender roles. A similar resistance to change situ-ation was faced by the many African American men who enlisted in America's military and had served their country during World War II and assumed they would return to find a nation ready to embrace racial equality, both political and economic. But this did not come to pass. It was the civil rights movement of the 1950s and 1960s that finally gave African Americans voting rights in the

The Great Depression of the 1930s caused economic devastation and social dislocation for millions of Americans. President Franklin Roosevelt responded to the crisis with a series of economic programs that were collectively referred to as the New Deal and were implemented to restore security. The New Deal programs led to the establishment and widespread acceptance of a greater role for government in the affairs of the economy for many decades thereafter. *(Wikipedia)*

South, and subsequent national legislation was needed to prohibit discrimination in the workplace.

Immediately after the end of World War II, there were efforts to dismantle and reverse New Deal provisions and legislation, including those laws and regulations that had secured greater labor rights. But the New Deal's undergirding principles carried over into what came to be known as the *Great Society* of the 1960s, first under President John F. Kennedy but especially under his successor, Lyndon B. Johnson. Great Society programs were initiated during a time of prosperity and focused numerous social issues. They included a war on poverty, federal funding to improve education, and health care programs for the elderly (Medicare) and for the poor (Medicaid). But it was also focused on fixing the longstanding problems arising from racial inequality. The Civil Rights Act of 1964 outlawed discrimination in employment and public services, and the Voting Rights Act of 1965 supported minority registration and voting.

The Reagan-Thatcher Revolution and the Return to Laissez-Faire

Political support for government alignment with the principles of the New Deal and Great Society programs began to wane during the 1970s, and opposition soon became bolder and better organized. The 1970s was a decade marked by a loss of confidence in U.S. business as goods from Europe and Japan flooded U.S. markets as vigorous and serious competition to American-made products. Confidence continued to spiral as Americans dealt with the oil embargo and rising oil prices, slow economic growth, and rising inflation.

Emerging from this pessimistic and cautious economic and political environment was movement that led back to earlier principles of neoclassical laissez-faire economics, a movement endorsed and rejuvenated by two strong-willed individuals with similar philosophies—President Ronald Reagan of the United States and Prime Minister Margaret Thatcher of the United Kingdom. The 1980s decade has, in fact, been referred to as the Reagan–Thatcher revolution. In many respects, their political philosophies reflected the views of economist Milton Friedman's 1962 classic, *Capitalism and Freedom*. Both leaders became champions of renewed faith in free markets and individualism. And although their actions did not quite match their rhetoric, both made substantial strides in advancing their agenda. They influenced government policy toward substantial business deregulation, or the loosening up or elimination of rules governing business activity, which they envisioned would permit greater freedom of business activity, and hence, greater overall prosperity. They advocated for reduced taxation, particularly with respect to corporations and wealthy investors, with the belief that this would encourage greater business investment activity that would eventually "trickle down" to benefit everyday workers and the country at large.

The 1980s has been referred to as the era of the Reagan–Thatcher revolution, named after U.S. President Ronald Reagan and Britain's Prime Minister Margaret Thatcher. Both leaders were powerful orators who advocated renewed faith in free markets and individualism, and a rejection of New Deal, Keynesian-style state planning and intervention into the economy. *(Getty)*

The Reagan–Thatcher revolution also tapped into particularly American cultural beliefs about individualism, as both leaders advocated for less government intervention into the affairs of the people, and more personal initiative, responsibility, and creativity in solving problems and creating a positive future. Within this context, American business was emboldened to rewrite the widely accepted employment compact with the American workforce, which had come to emphasize stability, security, and mutual prosperity throughout much of the twentieth century. In many respects, their legacy endured. Today, as we mentioned, individuals are encouraged to take control of their own careers, as permanent long-term secure employment awaits a smaller proportion of the workforce. As a corollary, union representation is at an all time low in the private sector, as the weakening of union power has enabled the movement towards greater business flexibility. Today, we are all encouraged to engage in continuous learning and career development, so that we can best be prepared for economic challenges that await us in the future.

Finally, the Reagan–Thatcher revolution was accompanied by major transformations in the world economy itself. Many other countries moved to privatize state-owned industries during the 1980s, deregulating their economies to permit the free flow of business activity within and across borders. This new global vision for the world political economy, known as *Neoliberalism*, reflected a return to early principles of classical liberal democracy: freedom, individualism, the capitalist market, and minimal state intervention into the economy. However, none of these changes had the power to do away with the large and powerful corporations and global investors that now span the globe in search of profits.

The Keynesian institutions and philosophy, which had informed the New Deal during the 1930s great depression and continued to thrive in the Great Society of the 1960s, were much weakened, with only a few features remaining fully intact (for instance, Social Security and Medicare). It was President Bill Clinton who probably best assessed the economic and political mood of the times with his 1996 comment, "The era of big government is over."

Notwithstanding former president Clinton's remarks about the end of big government, big government persists and is routinely scrutinized and criticized from many angles. Perhaps the only area of government that has not undergone major public scrutiny by critics over recent decades has been the area of defense and security, something easy to understand given the national homeland security concerns after September 11, 2001, and the subsequent military involvements in Iraq and Afghanistan. In connection with U.S. military operations in these two countries alone, government spending has skyrocketed during the past decade, albeit with increased use of private corporate contractors being favored over U.S. military personnel.

The State and Politics Today: Everyday Citizens Confront a Global Elite

Today the United States is still struggling to recover from the most serious financial crisis since the Great Depression. People continue to cope with the aftermath—an extended recession with high unemployment and the prospect of very slow job creation over the foreseeable future. And if we think about the path that led to this recession, it is easy to recall the quote cited in the beginning of this chapter in which the former chief economist of the IMF raised alarming concerns about the power of financial interests to influence the government's (inadequate) response to the financial crisis of 2007–2008, the crisis which drove the country into the recession that we continue to struggle with.

Johnson's analysis seems to imply that everyday citizens are not much of a political match against a financial elite in an era of neoliberal globalization. We might add that the same holds true for a once strong and now weakened countervailing power, which is unable to challenge the neoliberal view of how the future is to be framed.

In fact, the financial elite today co-exists with a fabulously affluent global elite, as pointed out by Chrystia Freeland in "The Rise of the New Global Elite," an article written for *The Atlantic*. Freeland notes that the widening gap between the wealthy and everyone else has been apparent for many years now. This view was driven home a few years ago by the widely publicized statements made by some business analysts at the giant Citigroup, a financial services company. These analysts remarked that the world is dividing into two blocs, "the plutonomy and the rest." They go onto state that

> In a plutonomy there is no such animal as "the U.S. consumer" or "the UK consumer" or indeed the "Russian consumer." There are rich consumers, few in number, but disproportionate in the gigantic slice of income and consumption they take. There are the rest, the "non-rich," the multitudinous many, but only accounting for surprisingly small bites of the national pie.

Perhaps the good news about today's global elite is that many of them acquired their fortunes the hard way, by earning it. That is, through hard work, creativity, and determination, they rose to the pinnacle of success in the global economy. The bad news is that they seem to have little sympathy for those who have not fared so well or are struggling economically. In fact the fortunes of the elite today now hinge increasingly upon a global workforce as opposed to one that is situated in their home countries. Therefore, they have little direct interest in the economic struggles of their fellow middle class citizens, not to mention those on the lower rungs of the societal ladder. In fact, if we consider the case of the United States, these elites are more likely to make a somewhat convincing argument that those with sufficient skills to match their countrymen and women in the global labor market, and who are willing to work for a fraction of the wages, deserve to be employed just as much, if not more, than do the more comfortable educated workers in the United States. If you are, or aspire to become, middle class one day, it seems that a bargain has already been struck with you—one that you and your parents may feel you had little part in negotiating. However, armed with a neoliberal worldview, which is reinforced by our longstanding and uniquely American beliefs about individualism, liberty, private property, and freedom, these elites would likely not see any bargain to be struck in the first place: just isolated individuals, buying, selling, and trading private property, protected by the full force and backing of the state, nothing more, nothing less. And so, if we wish to chart a more promising and hopeful path into the future, one that views the country (and the world for that matter) and its citizens are part of a somewhat larger interconnected whole, and which also takes into account the realities of concentrated wealth and power, we may need to draw upon renewed visions of political economy that offer alternatives to the reigning Neoliberal creed.

LOOKING AHEAD

In the following chapter, we will continue our discussion of major social institutions today. First, we will explore the changing nature of family and close personal relationships, especially as these have undergone dramatic transformation since the great transformation to modernity. Next, we will explore the institution of religion, which has experienced a dramatic diversification of formal religions practiced in society today, even as the broader role of religion in the modern world has been dramatically scaled back. We will also examine the emerging focus on spirituality as somewhat distinct from more traditional organized religious institutions.

Further Reading

Bellah. Robert N., Richard Madsen, William M. Sullivan, Ann Swidler, and Steven M. Tipton. *The Good Society.* New York: Alfred A. Knopf, 1991.

Bratton, John, David Denham, and Linda Deutschmann. *Capitalism and Classical Sociological Theory.* Toronto: University of Toronto Press, 2009.

Freeland, Chrystia. "The Rise of the New Global Elite." *The Atlantic.* January/February, 2011.

Friedman, Milton. *Capitalism and Freedom.* Chicago: University of Chicago Press, 1962.

Graham, Laurie. *On the Line at Subaru-Isuzu: The Japanese Model and the American Worker.* Ithaca, N.Y.: Cornell University Press, 1995.

Johnson, Simon. "The Quiet Coup." *The Atlantic.* May, 2009.

Kivisto, Peter. *Key Ideas in Sociology,* 2nd ed. Thousand Oaks, Calif.: Pine Forge, 2004.

Macionis, John J. *Society: The Basics.* 10th edition. Upper Saddle River, N.J.: Prentice Hall, 2009.

Parker, Richard. *John Kenneth Galbraith: His Life, His Politics, His Economics.* New York: Farrar, Straus, and Giroux, 2005.

Ritzer, George. *The McDonaldization of Society:* Thousand Oaks, Calif.: Pine Forge/Sage, 1993.

Uchitelle, Louis. *The Disposable American.* New York: Alfred A. Knopf, 2006.

Womack, James P., Daniel T. Jones, and Daniel Roos. *The Machine that Changed the World.* New York: Rawson Associates, 1990.

CHAPTER 5

THE INSTITUTIONAL CONTEXT II: FAMILY AND RELIGION

If you were a woman reading this magazine 40 years ago, the odds were good that your husband provided the money to buy it. That you voted the same way he did. That if you got breast cancer, he might be asked to sign the form authorizing a mastectomy. That your son was heading to college but not your daughter. That your boss, if you had a job, could explain that he was paying you less because, after all, you were probably working just for pocket money.

It's funny how things change slowly, until the day we realize they've changed completely. It's expected that by the end of the year, for the first time in history the majority of workers in the U.S. will be women—largely because the downturn has hit men so hard. This is an extraordinary change in a single generation, and it is gathering speed: The growth prospects, according to the Bureau of Labor Statistics, are in typically female jobs like nursing, retail and customer service. More and more women are the primary breadwinner[s] in their household[s] (almost 40 percent) or are providing essential income for the family's bottom line. Their buying power has never been greater—and their choices have seldom been harder.

This quote was from "What Women Want Now," an article written by Nancy Gibbs and published in the October 14, 2009, issue of *Time* magazine. The theme of the article revisits a classic *Time* article from 1972, which was titled "Where She Is and Where She's Going" and chronicled the state of what was then called the "new feminism" and the push for women's equality. The 2009 article points out just how much has changed over the past 40 years, with many of the changes occurring slowly and painfully, until we realize that the changes are complete and irreversible. The movement toward equality has involved dramatic changes in women's roles, mirrored by changing attitudes in society about the proper roles for women. Furthermore, this revolution in women's roles has been taking place on a worldwide scale, affecting all people—men, women, and children— albeit in different ways and at differing rates of change, depending upon the specific place and region of the world under consideration.

A central institution for which this transformation has had major implications is that of the family. In addition to accommodating new roles for women, which has been accompanied by some measure of adaptation by men, the family has experienced other related and powerful changes. Two of these are responses to economic developments associated with the great transformation to modernity, and in our more recent history a growing shift towards greater individualism.

Moreover, as we shall explore later in this chapter, similar and dramatic transformations have taken place in the institutions of religion in society. Clearly changes in both institutions are signaled by changes in women's roles. However, fundamental changes have also occurred in the meaning and power of these institutions to shape, guide, and direct the values, beliefs, and actions of individuals in the modern world. Of particular relevance to the changing power and significance of family and religion in society, has been the changing role of the *individual* in the transformation to modernity. Increasingly, people's lives have moved ever further from the confines of inherited customs, traditions and cultural beliefs, which historically cast them into ascribed roles (or status role-complexes), toward individualized lives and biographies that are today more open ended and brimming with alternative measures of creative potential, on the one hand, and insecurity and risk on the other.

Today the institutional signals emanating from our everyday cultural understandings of family and religion are neither simple and clear nor direct. This can be compared to the way we respond to traffic lights: When the signal is red or green, we know exactly what action is expected of us. However, when the light turns yellow, we have to make choices, and these may involve seizing an opportunity to move forward or slowing down and coming to a stop. With choice comes the benefit of individual freedom to make a decision but also the risk of exercising poor judgment. For many people today, the societal institutions of family and religion no long provide a clear set of bright red and solid green signals to follow. Instead, there are many yellow flashing lights, which on the one hand mean that individuals have greater opportunities to craft their involvement in each to reflect their unique values and commitments, and on the other hand mean they must exercise greater care and have an awareness of themselves and others to do this successfully. Furthermore, as a society we are still struggling to comprehend how these institutions themselves are evolving and learning to make adaptations that will better meet the needs of individuals and of the collective society.

FAMILY AS A SOCIAL INSTITUTION

Although there are several ways to define family, we will start with sociologist Susan J. Ferguson's broad definition of this institution. In her book *Shifting the Center: Understanding Contemporary Families* Ferguson writes that "family as a social institution provides three things: (1) it gives support to its members (whether it be emotional nurturing, physical caretaking, economic support, or some combination of the three); (2) it binds the individual to a primary group . . . ; and (3) it socializes the person for participating in society outside of the family."

Sociologist John J. Macionis, in his introductory textbook *Society: The Basics*, discusses the concept of **kinship**, which refers to "a social bond based on common ancestry, marriage, or adoption." In addition, he points out that while all societies contain families, those individuals or groups that people define as kin has varied historically as well as cross-culturally. Today, families commonly (but certainly not exclusively) coalesce around a **marriage**, a "legal relationship, usually involving economic cooperation, sexual activity, and childbearing."

Macionis also defines core functions or purposes associated with family that are quite similar to those identified by Susan Ferguson. For instance, he points out the importance of family (and especially of parents) as the first and primary agents of *socialization* for children. Successful socialization generally means that children will gradually be integrated into the larger society and become contributing members of that society. Furthermore, a historical function of families has been to *regulate the sexual activity* of their members, with every culture adopting some version of the **incest taboo**. This is a norm that forbids sexual relations and/or marriage between certain relatives. Social scientists believe that it serves to limit sexual competition within the family and among kin, thus strengthening cooperation; it helps to maintain the social order provided by the kinship system; and finally, it serves to prevent genetic or mental/physical damage to offspring. Other functions of families include providing *material* (which could be physical or financial) *and emotional security and support*, as well as *social placement*. Families generally pass on their *social identities* to their children, including their race, ethnicity, religion, and social class. In fact, critics of the family point out how the institution is a vehicle that perpetuates inequality throughout society because it passes down social class privileges or disadvantages as well as racial and ethnic divisions from generation to generation.

Family in Historical Context

In thinking about how today's families function, the purposes they serve, what we value about them, and why we might be critical of them, it is important to understand the institution in historical context. It is also important to understand the social foundations upon which family was first established and how those social foundations have also evolved and changed. In his book *Runaway World: How Globalization is Reshaping Our Lives*, social theorist Anthony Giddens explains just how dramatically the social foundations upon which the institution of family has rested have shifted over the last several centuries. He traces these shifts through development of the modern world (which we have described as the great transformation to modernity) and to what he refers to as today's era of late or second modernity.

The Traditional Family

During the past few decades, women in Western industrialized nations made great strides towards full equality in society, and the new individualism promised expanded freedom and choice for the individual. At the same time this was occurring, many were disturbed and unsettled by these changes and began

Peasants in Russia. The traditional family has historically been an economically productive unit involving extended familial relations, in which children are understood to be useful and productive assets to the larger collective family enterprise, and where, in many cases, arranged marriages have been the norm. *(Library of Congress)*

to call for a return to the traditional family. Giddens points out, however, that contemporary society generally holds misguided images about the true historical nature of this "traditional" family. First and foremost, few people are aware that the *traditional family* was a productive economic unit that involved the entire family group. Giddens draws examples from Europe during medieval times, when a preindustrial agrarian way of life was the norm. In that world, sexual or romantic love was not the basis for marriage. Marriage was, in fact, an economic and hierarchical construct with a very clear set of social rules. Social inequality, for example, was a built-in feature of the traditional family—women and children were subservient to men and, in many societies, legally defined as property. In this world, sexuality served one primary function—reproduction. The children born into these marriages were expected to contribute to the common productive economic enterprise undertaken by the larger family, which invariably meant agricultural labor.

Giddens also points out that traditional and more modern versions of family do co-exist in some contemporary societies today. He notes, for instance, how China's great Cultural Revolution greatly liberalized marriage laws and made divorce easy. These legal and cultural changes, implemented several decades ago, continue to influence urban life in China. He notes, in contrast, that marriage and family life in China's rural areas is more traditional and that *arranged marriages*, where parents select marriage partners for their children, are still fairly common in some provinces.

The 1950s Breadwinner–Homemaker Ideal

Giddens notes that many of those who long for a "return to the traditional family" are really looking back at the idealized "traditional family" of the 1950s. But this decade was a period of transition away from the traditional family form and that transition was well underway. By the 1950s family era—captured so perfectly today on the TV Land channel with old reruns of "Leave it to Beaver"—companionship and romantic love had already begun to replace the earlier (and more exacting) traditional compact as the basis for marriage. Nonetheless, there are reasons that we tend to think of the 1950s as an era of the traditional family. One of these reasons is that marriage at that time was defined by the *breadwinner–homemaker* model, with men and women inhabiting separate spheres and taking on ascribed gender roles. In this ideal, male breadwinners were primarily responsible for providing for their families through wage labor in the formal capitalist economy. Women, on the other hand, were responsible for the domestic front, which meant running the household, raising and nurturing the children, and caring for their husbands. Furthermore, the *nuclear family*, with parents and children residing together in a shared household separate from other kin, had come to be the norm by the 1950s, eclipsing the traditional model that included a wider range of kin in a "family" household.

The Couple Today

In many respects, the 1950s family existed as a transition phase in family life, but this model continues to have some measure of cultural significance even today. As Giddens notes, however, it is the *couple* that is the major focus of intimate relationships today, primarily because sexuality is no longer tied strictly to reproduction, and is certainly not exclusively expressed within the institution of marriage. The maintenance of the couple relationship today depends upon active trust, emotional communication, and intimacy between partners. When couples form families, they may or may not choose to have children. Viewed in contrast to the traditional family, where children were viewed as productive assets who contributed to the household economy (the farm), children in contemporary families have become economic liabilities because raising them in today's world can be very expensive. In addition to providing food, (fashionable) clothing, and shelter, many parents also invest a good deal of money in extracurricular activities, consumer goods, and college tuition. Thus, the decision to have children is no longer based on economic necessity; it is, instead, a decision based on desire, sometimes tempered by financial considerations. Those who choose to have children often do so to meet psychological and emotional needs.

As an interesting corollary to this, Giddens points out that today's families are implicitly democratic institutions in which respect, dialog and mutual trust have led to greater equality among partners, something which has also been extended in significant measure to children. In preindustrial, agrarian traditional families, the father's will was law; women and children were often considered chattel. In today's democratic family, parents (and this includes women) are charged with making the final decisions, but children are increasingly permitted to answer back, raise questions, ask for justifications, and suggest alternatives.

Public and Private Families

One leading family sociologist, Andrew Cherlin, contends that understanding and making sense of the changing nature of the family requires two separate definitions that capture (in tandem) their diverse composition, modes of organization, as well as the myriad of purposes or functions that they serve. For Cherlin, the first definition is the *Public Family* and refers to the older traditional notion of family that emphasized caring for children and other dependents, such as the frail elderly, as well as the contributions that families make towards advancing the needs of society. This definition focuses on financial provision and physical support, along with roles, commitments and obligations to the common needs of the larger family group and society. In contrast is the *private family*, which defines and emphasizes the coming together of people who share intimate relations within a shared household supported by pooled resources, but whose primary purpose is to provide love and meet the emotional needs of individual members within that household. In this private form, individuals place great emphasis on emotional fulfillment and gratification, and the members who make up the family can include a range of individuals who are not necessarily kin, but who freely choose to care about one another. Children may or may not be included in the private family. The decision to have children is a personal one, and is not necessarily part of a wider commitment to the broader community.

More recently, Cherlin has spoken of the *deinstitutionalization of marriage*, by which he means that the everyday taken-for-granted norms that define the expectations placed upon participants in this institution have been weakened to such an extent that individuals have a hard time defining them, let alone relying upon them. Within this confusing and amorphous framework, they must constantly negotiate how to take action in a myriad of situations. Several transformations are relevant for understanding this phenomenon. For instance, with the increase in the number of wives leaving the home every day to participate in the labor force came the need to revise the taken-for-granted assumptions of the breadwinner–homemaker model. And although men have assumed some of the housework because women are working outside the home and not only in the home, most couples find that they must work out their own negotiations about domestic division of labor because no clear set of social norms has emerged to provide adequate guidance. Another trend that Cherlin identifies has been the increase in childbearing outside of marriage. By 1980, one child in six was born out of wedlock; by the mid-2000s, this ratio had changed to roughly 1 out of 3. Clearly, marriage no longer represents the sole context in which childbearing takes place.

Another major transformation contributing to the deinstitutionalization of marriage is the rise of *cohabitation*, or two people living together and sharing an intimate relationship outside of marriage. Demographer Kathleen Kiernan notes how cohabitation is often accepted by society in stages. These stages begin with cohabitation being viewed as a highly circumspect practice occurring on the fringes of society. Next, it is accepted as a testing ground for marriage. After that, it becomes an acceptable alternative to marriage, and finally it becomes indistinguishable from marriage. Cherlin sees evidence that the United States seems to be in a transition between viewing cohabitation as a testing ground for marriage and an acceptable alternative to marriage.

Both Cherlin and Giddens point out how this element of personal choice is most fully explored through the rise of same-sex marriage. Lesbian and gay couples who are able to marry—and the legal definition of marriage is still subject to ongoing debates at both the state and federal levels of government in the United States—must actively construct the norms of the marriage with the least amount of institutional guidance. Furthermore, Cherlin notes how gays and lesbians have been more inclined to include a wider range of individuals, especially those chosen voluntarily as opposed to being related by blood, into their personal definitions of family.

In the end, Cherlin asks, "Why do people still marry?" Given the current context for marriage in which individuals exercise high levels of personal choice in shaping the institution, and in which individuals are more likely to demand that in order for a marriage to remain viable it must continually meet their expectations for personal fulfillment, perhaps the institution is headed for eventual demise. Cherlin notes, however, that surveys of high school seniors have continually indicated strong support for the institution over recent decades, with roughly 80 percent of women responding that they expect to marry some day, the expectations of young men queried on this matter having increased over the same time period from about 71 percent to 78 percent.

Cherlin concludes that while the practical significance of marriage seems to have declined over the past several decades, its symbolic significance has remained high. He cites, for example, a major survey of adults aged 20 to 29, which indicates that marriage is a valued status that one works toward achieving. Responses to survey questions also indicate that these respondents value successful marriages, meaning that individuals should seriously explore their compatibility (say, through living together, an option supported by 62 percent of those responding) before marrying, and that they should make sure to be "economically set" prior to getting married (supported by 82 percent). However, the most important ingredient in marriage, according to those participating in the survey, is intimacy and love. Among those who had never married, over 90 percent agreed that "when you marry, you want your spouse to be your soul mate, first and foremost." Marriage, it appears, continues to hold high symbolic and personal significance as means of personal achievement and fulfillment among young adults.

Diversity and Family: African Americans and Latinos

The United States is often referred to as a nation of immigrants, with a high degree of racial, ethnic, and religious diversity. In this section we briefly explore ways in which diversity in the American context has implications for family life today for two major minority groups: Hispanic Latinos and African Americans. For some time now, the fastest growing racial or ethnic minority population in the United States has been Hispanic Latinos, who account for roughly fifteen percent of the population. Members of this rapidly growing ethnic group actually come from many different countries in Latin America, with Mexican Americans making up well over half of this population, followed by Puerto Rican Americans and Cuban Americans.

Because Hispanic Latino Americans identify with a wide range of countries of origin, they constitute a rather diverse U.S. ethnic group. However, there are certain characteristics that are commonly associated with Hispanic Latino

Americans, some of which we might associate with the traditional families described by Anthony Giddens. These characteristics include a wider range of involvement with and mutual support and commitment to extended kin. With this comes greater involvement and active interest among parents in rituals of courtship and marriage between children. Moreover, traditional gender roles within the family are emphasized to a great extent. But these characteristics, which involve a great emphasis on *familism*, or a focus on the needs and interests of the wider family group over those of the individual, are certainly undergoing transformation for Hispanic Latinos in the United States. One indicator of this is that many Hispanic Latina women in this country are having fewer children than their mothers did, and in some respects, their families are not as deeply involved with extended kin relations, a change that reflects the struggle to balance the values and traditions that have defined family life over generations with the individualistic culture and distinctive institutional context of U.S. society.

The average annual income both for both Hispanic Latino families and African American families is less than 70 percent of the average for white families in the United States. African American families in particular have labored

When Barack Obama took office in January 2009, the Obamas became the first African American First Family. The family's unique historic role, set against the backdrop of the turbulent legacy of race relations in the United States, has sparked great interest, and almost every aspect of the First Family experience has been exposed to intense cultural and political scrutiny in the mass media. *(Wikipedia)*

under a historical legacy of slavery, followed by historical patterns of racism, prejudice and discrimination. Today, African American families have the highest rates of single, female-headed households (over 40 percent), a family form that is highly associated with poverty. And while this family form has been increasing among other minority groups (as well as within the majority white population), its prevalence among African Americans has been associated with an especially high degree of social scrutiny.

Scholars have vigorously debated the historical evidence used to reconstruct family patterns among African Americans in the past. Some point to a rich historical legacy of West African family traditions valuing women's productive work and female-centered kinship. They emphasize how this heritage has fostered resiliency among African American families headed by single mothers, who are engaged in flexible networks of exchange and reciprocity. Others have argued that the (1950s ideal) heterosexual nuclear family has historically been the dominant form among African Americans, but that racism has made it more difficult for African Americans to reproduce this family form. In the end, however, it is important to note that African American families are rather diverse and do not fit a one-dimensional profile of family form, family ideals, and class background.

Divorce, Remarriage, and Blended Families

As family sociologist Andrew Cherlin's survey showed, even though marriage in America seems to be going through a process of deinstitutionalization there is still strong support for the institution among young adults. Oddly enough, this embrace of marriage coincides with a high prevalence of divorce. Not so oddly, however, divorce has contributed to high rates of remarriage. Over the past century, divorce has gone from being an extremely rare occurrence to a common practice, to the point where roughly four in ten marriages now end in divorce. There are numerous potential causes and reasons for this. Many of these should not be surprising, particularly given our discussion of Giddens's focus on the centrality of the couple relationship (rather than the family relationship) and the related discussion on Cherlin's identification of the shift from a public to private understanding of family.

Some of the main causes of divorce include greater focus on individualism and personal fulfillment, which can lead individuals to terminate marriages that they find unfulfilling or marriages in which romantic love and intimacy have waned. Furthermore, divorce has become more socially acceptable and easier to obtain than in times past. Other factors are related to the changing gender roles in marriage, especially in *dual-earner families*, where both spouses work in the paid labor force and face stressors associated with juggling the complex demands of work and family. Related to these stressors is what sociologist Arlie Hochschild, in her book *The Second Shift*, refers to as the "stalled revolution."

The highly successful television comedy series *Modern Family* depicts the complex familial relations that have evolved between a father, his adult children, and their respective families. The father is divorced, remarried, and now has a stepson. His daughter is in a heterosexual marriage and has three biological children; his son is in a gay marriage, and the couple recently adopted a daughter. In its own idiosyncratic manner, the show humorously embraces late-modern themes of love, intimacy, and commitment, as well as mutual concern and respect. *(Photofest)*

The book's title refers to the housework and child care that must be attended to by dual-earning couples after the paid work day has finished. The stalled revolution refers to the fact that on average husbands have increased the amount of time they spend doing housework and child care as wives have come to spend more time in the paid labor force, but the major burden of the second shift still falls primary on the wives. The relational conflict that this imbalance generates in marriages has been a major source of divorce. Finally, now that many women do earn substantial incomes, and increasingly breadwinner wages, in the paid labor force, they are no longer simply dependent upon husbands for their survival and may therefore feel less compelled to stay in unhappy, unfair, or abusive relationships.

Regardless of the reasons for divorce, a majority of those who divorce end up remarrying within five years, which means that half of all marriages in the United States are second marriages for at least one partner. Remarriages then lead to the formation of *blended families*, which can include combinations of biological parents and stepparents, as well as brothers, sisters, and half-siblings. While blended families do offer opportunities for individuals to forge new types of kin relations, they also pose new challenges in terms of defining just who belongs in one's family, and what kinds of responsibilities individuals (be they parents, children, or relatives) have toward one another.

Social Class and Childrearing

Because Americans value individual achievement and success in U.S. society, most believe that the class system should be open and fluid. By this, we generally mean that any individual should have the opportunity to achieve a measure of success through hard work and personal initiative. We also know that family plays an important role in the opportunities that children have in life. Families with the means to do so can provide their children will rich educational experiences and support them in preparing for admission to and attendance at university, which is an extremely expensive proposition for today's young adults.

Beyond what we refer to as the material or financial benefits that parents are able to confer upon their children, there are also cultural and social benefits that children acquire primarily due to their parents' social class background, which is often linked to the community in which they live and where they go to school. Sociologist Annette Lareau describes how upper middle class parents with university degrees and managerial or professional jobs foster a growing sense of entitlement to their children. These parents tend to be actively involved in assessing and then nurturing their children's talents and skills. Such parents often reason with their children, permitting them to raise questions and negotiate parental advice or directives. In doing so, they encourage children to express themselves verbally and engage in complex reasoning. Finally, they regularly communicate on their children's behalf with authority figures at institutions regularly or sporadically attended by their children (e.g., schools, doctors' office, etc.). They are comfortable negotiating and communicating as equals with these authority figures and encourage their children to do the same. Over time their children develop a growing sense of confidence and even entitlement in their dealings with such institutions and their representatives.

In contrast, Lareau notes that working-class parents, who have a limited education (typically high school) and who work as janitors, welders, bus drivers, assemblers, and in similar occupations (including lower level retail service jobs), take a rather different approach to childrearing. These parents tend to allow their children to grow and develop naturally—they seldom intervene in their daily lives and activities, except when issuing directives. In contrast to upper middle class parents, working-class parents tend to issue clear directives to their children, and these directives are generally not questioned. There is little room for negotiation or dialog or explanation, and children are not encouraged to develop extensive verbal skills through their interactions with parents.

Moreover, working-class parents tend to approach outside institutions with some hesitation, even viewing them with suspicion. They are not entirely comfortable interacting with authority figures in schools or at doctors' offices and may even feel a tension between their own values and childrearing practices at home and the expectations of authority figures in those institutions. The tenuous and somewhat distrustful relationship with these outside authority figures sometimes results in feelings of powerlessness and frustration that children gradually come to internalize and experience themselves.

Working Families and Economic Risk

Aside from the traditional advantages or constraints that affect children from different class backgrounds and circumstances, is a set of institutional shifts over recent decades that has affected most families in the United States (regardless of status and class standing). These shifts have created and enabled an environment of economic risk. Moreover, this phenomenon has had a cumulative effect that intensifies the sense of risk. In *The Great Risk Shift*, published in 2006, political scientist Jacob Hacker sounded a clear warning on this matter, noting that everyday families have been experiencing increasing levels of economic risk over the past generation. One major theme in the institutional shift that has led to this state of affairs, Hacker points out, is that corporate/business leaders have been advocating that Americans adopt increasingly individualized solutions for a wide range of social and institutional problems. In so doing, the corporate elite has managed to offload responsibility for managing a range of economic risks from business and government onto individuals and families. This is particularly the case with respect to three major (and interconnected) issues: employment security, retirement, and health care.

Hacker and others note that profitable corporations once made an implicit compact with their full-time workers, which involved a sense of loyalty and a long-term commitment running both ways. Today, those who work to provide for their families increasingly find that they cannot count on having secure long-term employment. Indeed, the growing trend in many business is hiring part-time, temporary, and contract employees at lower wages and with fewer (if any) benefits. Another way in which families have been made less secure by the current economic environment has been the movement away from (and perhaps more accurately, the abandoning of) once clearly defined benefit retirement pensions plans. In the past, these plans rewarded long-term employees with a fixed monthly income (or retirement benefit) until death. Finally (and very much related to the end of long-term employment security and the growing trend toward part-time workers) is the growing number of Americans who do not get adequate health insurance benefits from their employers.

On a related front, legal scholar Elizabeth Warren and others have been documenting increasing incidences of middle-class bankruptcy over the past generation—a roughly fivefold increase in the last twenty-five years. She notes how the most common cause of bankruptcy is devastating illness and medical expenses that destroy the family budget. Warren further notes that in the majority of bankruptcies involving medical expenses, the families concerned actually had health insurance but that their coverage was limited in some way.

Warren's interest in the bankruptcy crisis is not solely academic. The co-author of *The Two-Income Trap* has also been one of the leading advocates for families who have been financially devastated by credit card debt or extremely risky home mortgage loans over recent years. In connection with this work, she has pointed out how a weakening of government rules and regulations regarding interest rates has led to predatory business practices among credit card companies and mortgage lenders over the years. These particular issues certainly came to a head with the recent bursting of the housing bubble and subsequent financial crisis. As a result of this crisis, the United States has been experiencing high levels of unemployment, job loss, and record high home foreclosure rates.

RELIGION AS A SOCIAL INSTITUTION

Having explored how families are evolving in contemporary society and the pressures influencing changes in this institution, we now turn to the institution of religion, which has also undergone dramatic change in the modern era. We begin with the assertion that religion continues to be intertwined with family in very significant ways. For instance, many core rituals and rites of passage that involve the institution of family are either directly or indirectly defined through religion. Rituals associated with birth, especially baptism, are oftentimes drawn from religious sources, as are those connected to marriage and death, through the rituals of weddings and funerals respectively.

Religion was an important source of study and interest among the founders of sociology. One of the most important founders, French sociologist Emile Durkheim, was a pioneer in the sociology of religion over a century ago. He postulated that religion played a central role in the early advancement of society and formed the basis for the later development of scientific knowledge by generating basic categories of thought, including time, space, and force, among others. Durkheim theorized how religious beliefs of early societies divided their worlds into two opposing realms or domains: the sacred and the profane. The domain of the **sacred** contains elements, objects, ideas, people, etc., that are set apart from the rest of the social world and inspire awe and reverence. The realm of the **profane** is defined as outside of, or set apart from, the sacred. It involves the ordinary elements of the everyday social world. In his now classic work, *The Elementary Forms of Religious Life*, Durkheim defined **religion** as "a unified system of beliefs and practices relative to sacred things, that is to say, things set apart and surrounded by prohibitions—beliefs and practices that unite its adherents in a single moral community called a church." The sacred is often embodied in **rites** or **rituals**, which can be thought of as formal ceremonial behavior involving the sacred.

Early sociologists, including Durkheim, were also concerned with what they viewed as the decline of community and tradition accompanying the rise of modern society. Recall, for example, our earlier discussion in Chapter 2 of Charles H. Cooley and his emphasis on society shifting away from primary toward secondary groups. In Durkheim's case, however, this decline was also linked to a diminished role for religion in the modern world, a phenomenon that was occurring through a process of secularization, especially in his native Europe. In observing this phenomenon, Durkheim theorized that the sacred persists in modernity, but it does so in a radically new way. He argued that the modern world produces the *cult of the individual*. With modernity, according to Durkheim, society elevates the individual to a sacred status, endowing him (and increasingly her) with inalienable rights. He also foresaw that individualism in the modern world would evolve along one or two paths. The first path, reflective of what he called *moral individualism*, meant that the individual would be socialized by society to show concern and respect for others, given their sacred status. In contrast, Durkheim feared that the cult of the individual would simply lead to *egoism*, with the individual increasingly showing concern for self and personal selfish needs and desires at the expense of other individuals and the collective.

In spite of forecasts to the contrary among theorists of modernity, religion continues to persist in the contemporary world. Some of the core functions or purposes associated with the historically core institution of religion, according to Durkheim, are that it integrates the individual into the group, while it also regulates behavior among its members. Religion *integrates* or unites people in the group through the use of shared and powerful imagery, symbols, sacred objects, and the reaffirmation of shared values. When these are drawn upon in a ritualized context, such as a religious service, the effect can be one in which the individual feels an emotional-spiritual connection to the group and to their shared sense of the divine. By *regulation*, Durkheim further posited that religion also encourages, even demands, that individuals follow the established cultural norms and practices of the group. Members of a church may indeed be very conscious of how fellow parishioners and church leaders may respond to their behavior in the world. Furthermore, many religions define God as an ultimate and omniscient judge of the actions of its members, not to mention all people on earth, an interpretation that also serves as a source of regulation among believers.

Finally, as sociologist Peter Berger emphasizes in *The Sacred Canopy*, religion provides followers with a sense of meaning, purpose, and stability in life, particularly in the context of an unstable or uncertain world. In the current global age, world events, wars, natural disasters, and tragedies swirl around us

Sociologist Emile Durkheim believed that religion serves to integrate members into the life of the group and regulate their behavior. It also provides followers with a sense of meaning and purpose in life. (Wikipedia)

through the power of the mass media via Internet, television, newspapers, movies, etc. Within this maelstrom, religion provides many people with sense of comfort in the belief that there is a larger cosmic sense of meaning and divine guidance over their world and over the larger universe.

Major criticisms of religion have been that it is an institution that has traditionally supported and reinforced systems of *patriarchy*, reinforcing the dominant role of men and the subordination of women in society. In the Christian tradition, for instance, critics point to biblical teachings that instruct wives to be subordinate to their husbands, claiming that this reinforces women's traditional ascribed roles in society. Others (like Max Weber) point out that religious institutions often provide political legitimacy and support for the institutions of government and maintenance of the status quo in society. While this may be difficult for us to observe in modern, democratic societies like the United States, religion in Europe during earlier medieval times was closely integrated with the ruling governing powers in society. Even in the U.S. context, we can see that religion played a role in how slavery was perceived. Ironically, it provided justification for slavery in the Southern states while it simultaneously inspired the abolitionist movement. Nearly a century later, it played an important role in shaping the civil rights movement of the 1950s and 1960s.

Religion, the Enlightenment, and the Rise of Modernity

The fate of religion in the Western world was greatly impacted by two events: a period in European history known as the *Enlightenment* and the French Revolution of 1789. The French Revolution was a clear attack upon absolute monarchy and the divine right of kings, both of which were reinforced by the institution of the *feudal estate system* that had been in place throughout Europe since the middle ages. Under this system the Catholic Church wielded great power and influence. In this feudal-agrarian world, the church had accumulated great wealth through its extensive landholdings and also held great political legitimacy as it spoke with a claim to the authority of God. The *feudal aristocracy*, which was a hereditary nobility, was closely aligned with the church, and also claimed to rule by divine providence. Together the church and the ruling aristocracy were at the top of a hierarchical system of *estates*—the latter, particularly the monarch, occupying the first, and the church occupying the second. Below the first two estates, was a third estate consisting of peasants, commoners, and in some cases serfs (who were just above slaves in terms of their lack of freedoms and social standing), who made up the vast majority of the population, and enjoyed limited rights and privileges.

The French Revolution was clearly rooted in economic conflict, as the growing urban middle classes, especially the bourgeoisie (small merchants and traders), came to challenge the laws and privileges of the monarchy and wider aristocracy. But this revolution drew inspiration from the ideas of the

Enlightenment, just as Enlightenment philosophers drew inspiration from earlier advances in the natural sciences, for instance, the discoveries of Sir Isaac Newton, the development of Newtonian Physics, and his three laws of motion. Some of these philosophers came to believe in the possibility of a science of society, where the pursuit of scientific truth could liberate people from religious dogma or the divine right of kings. Guided in part by these ideas, the French

King Charles I. In Europe's predemocratic past, the feudal system was buttressed by a belief in the divine right of kings, which was reinforced by the authority of the Catholic Church. Supporters of the French Revolution drew inspiration from Enlightenment ideas, which held out the promise that science, along with free and rational inquiry, would help liberate people from autocratic rule and rigid religious dogma. *(Wikipedia)*

Revolution represented a challenge to the aristocratic state and the religious and political institutions that supported it.

With the growing power and presence of science as a legitimate system by which knowledge would be created and disseminated in society, a key issue emerged regarding the legitimacy of religious knowledge and its influence upon human affairs. Here, the growing ascendency of scientific knowledge meant that religious authorities had to compete with other sources of knowledge and understanding in the public sphere, sometimes claiming authority through divine revelation, but increasingly pointing to scientific support for their claims. In other instances, these advocates for maintaining the status quo pointed out how custom and tradition, rooted in the historical past, provided the best guidance for approaching an uncertain future.

Religious Belief and Affiliation in the U.S. Today

As noted above, despite predictions made by theorists of modernity, religion continues to persist in the contemporary world. In his 2009 work *Society*, sociologist John Macionis highlights survey research from the National Opinion Research Center (NORC), pointing out the ways in which Americans are, and are not, very religious. An analysis of responses to this survey showed that roughly 80 percent of adults in the United States claimed to gain "comfort and strength" from religion, and over 90 percent of Americans claimed to believe in a divine power. At the same time, slightly less than 65 percent of those surveyed claimed they "know God exists and have no doubts about." Furthermore, while almost 60 percent of adults said they pray at least once a day, only about 30 percent said they attend religious services on a weekly or almost weekly basis.

Roughly 85 percent of Americans identify with a specific religious tradition. Those belonging to Protestant denominations (Episcopalians, Presbyterians, Methodists, Baptists, and Lutherans, among others), make up more than half of all U.S. adults. Catholics make up roughly 25 percent of the population, and Jews account for about 2 percent. Over the past few decades, the number of Muslims in American society has increased, with many coming from the Middle East, where Islam is the dominant religion. The Hindu population has grown over recent decades as well, with the vast majority of Hindus tracing their lineage to India, a country with cultural influences deeply rooted in Hinduism.

In this discussion, it is important to underscore that the Christian church has played a historically central role in the lives of African Americans. When Africans were brought to the Americas on slave ships, they brought almost nothing tangible. But they did bring elements of their ancestral African religious traditions. Once in the Americas, African slaves adopted the dominant Christian religion, but they also transformed it into a distinctive form shaped by their ancient traditions. In this manifestation, the church became a major social institution in the lives of African Americans, fulfilling a wide range of functions to serve the needs of its members, who have long experienced racism, prejudice, and discrimination from majority institutions in society. More recently, some African Americans have embraced a wider range of faiths in addition to Christianity, with Islam being the most common among them.

Religion and Late Modernity

Much in keeping with the dominant trends associated with modernity, religious affiliation (as well as the nature of religious involvement) is characterized by change in contemporary U.S. society. For instance, survey evidence indicates that over 40 percent of Americans have changed religious affiliation at some point in their lives. Attendance at and affiliation with some Protestant churches have fallen by almost half over the last fifty years. As Macionis reports, it is estimated that one-third of Catholics have left the Catholic Church, but those numbers have been made up by others, mainly immigrants.

One major transformation associated with modernity has been increasing *secularization*, or the decline in importance of the sacred in social life. In connection with this, we are increasingly turning to formal scientific-professional experts in society to cope with a range of issues. Even many of those who consider themselves to be religious will turn to the medical establishment should a family member become ill, even though they may also offer prayers for good health. Or consider how many young adults still value the symbolic significance of marriage and being married in a church, even though the decision to marry may not involve more than passing consultation with a religious authority figure. Increasingly, the decision to take part in a religious community is a personal individual choice, involving little or no outside pressure. In fact, it would be downright illegal and discriminatory for one's employer to insist upon a certain form of religious observation, even as such pressures may persist in an informal manner in certain institutional contexts. For instance, there is seems to be an implicit understanding among U.S. presidential candidates that they must demonstrate outward signs of religious belief and affiliation with a specific (Christian) church.

Much along the lines of Durkheim's interest in secularization and modernity, sociologist Robert Bellah, whom we have discussed in various segments of this book, raises the importance of *civil religion* in the context of a secularizing society. By this Bellah refers to citizenship as a quasi-sacred responsibility placed upon members of society. He points out how with the rise of individualism in modern society, there is a constant danger that everyday citizens will grow passive, even apathetic, about the fate of our dominant institutions, and turn instead to the comforts and pleasure of private life, confined to a smaller group of family and friends. Bellah points out that the two major historical traditions of *biblical religion* and *civic republicanism*—the former being religious in nature and the latter being more secular—need to be continually reinvigorated with the energy, passion, and commitment of citizens to ensure that we maintain concern for our collective life and for the health of our institutions. He notes that through both of these traditions, citizens have taken part in the larger collective life of the community and society. In these public contexts, people meet one another face to face and in doing so, are aware of the larger social and institutional world that makes up society and that affords citizens the privilege of taking refuge in private life. In the process, these traditions have exerted a tempering influence on individualism.

With increasing levels of secularization in society, two final trends are worth noting. First, over recent decades, and much in line with the advancement of the institutions of modernity, there has been a growing movement among a segment of the population toward greater spirituality, and the seeking of spiritual growth, outside of the confines of traditional religious denominations. In fact, this movement, often referred to as *new age spirituality*, very much downplays any adherence to doctrine or dogma. Instead, its adherents tend to embrace a vague notion of a higher power, even as they tend to believe in a transcendent spiritual world. Much of their effort is directed at experiencing this transcendent spiritual reality, but they wish to do so in a manner that respects individual choice, tolerance of others, and religious pluralism.

Not surprisingly, while new age spirituality seems to be concerned with transcending more traditional historic notions of religion, another powerful religious movement, which has had powerful political influence in society over recent decades, is *fundamentalism*. This refers to a reactionary movement that seeks to restore traditional religious belief and practice against the forces of a secularizing modernity. While fundamentalism exists in all major religions, Southern Baptists represent the most active and powerful fundamentalist community in the United States. Fundamentalists tend to be suspicious of calls for religious pluralism and tolerance because they fear these might weaken personal faith. They also tend to be very wary and skeptical of the wider secular humanist world, a world made possible by the Enlightenment. Their criticisms of secular humanism are very much connected to a belief in the literal interpretation of the Bible (or other sacred texts, depending upon the religion) as the absolute word of God. This often leads fundamentalists to be wary of intellectuals, and to some extent the institutions of science, as these may challenge their fundamentalist beliefs in the nature of God, the universe, and human nature itself.

LOOKING AHEAD

In the following chapter we will take up two more important social institutions that are central to the modern world today, both of which can be viewed as offspring of modernity. We will first look at the institution of education, explore its growth and rising significance over the course of the past 150 years, and then take up some challenges facing this institution today. Next, we will explore the mass media, briefly describing its rise in the twentieth century and then more fully discussing its impact upon society today. Both institutions have distinctive roles in shaping, informing, and socializing individuals in the contemporary world, and both have implications for the way in which our families, the economy, and politics and government function today.

Further Reading

Bellah. Robert N., Richard Madsen, William M. Sullivan, Ann Swidler, and Steven M. Tipton. *The Good Society.* New York: Alfred A. Knopf, 1991.

Berger, Peter L. *The Sacred Canopy: Elements of a Sociological Theory of Religion.* Garden City, N.Y.: Doubleday, 1967.

Cherlin, Andrew J. "The Deinstitutionalization of American Marriage." *Journal of Marriage and the Family* 66 (2004):848–861.

_____. *Public and Private Families: An Introduction.* 5th ed. Boston: McGraw-Hill, 2008.

Durkheim, Emile. *The Elementary Forms of Religious Life.* New York: Free Press, [1915] 1965.

Ferguson, Susan J. *Shifting the Center: Understanding Contemporary Families.* 3rd ed. Boston: McGraw Hill, 2007.

Giddens, Anthony. Runaway World. New York: Routledge, 2000.

Hacker, Jacob S. *The Great Risk Shift: The Assault on American Jobs, Families, Health Care and Retirement And How You Can Fight Back.* Oxford: Oxford University Press, 2006.

Gibbs, Nancy. "What Women Want Now." *Time.* October 14, 2009.

Hochschild, Arlie R. *The Second Shift.* New York: Avon, 1989.

Macionis, John J. *Society: The Basics.* 10th ed. Upper Saddle River, N.J.: Prentice Hall, 2009.

Warren, Elizabeth, and Amelia Warren Tyagi. *The Two-Income Trap: Why Middle-Class Mothers and Fathers Are Going Broke.* New York: Basic Books, 2003.

CHAPTER 6

THE INSTITUTIONAL CONTEXT III: EDUCATION AND MASS MEDIA

Education has become something of a panacea for all social problems in the twentieth century. But instead of dumping our unsolved problems on our public schools or expecting our universities to come up with technical solutions to our difficulties, we should recover a more classical notion that it is the whole way of life that educates. Our jobs, our consumer marketplaces, our laws and our government agencies, our cities and neighborhoods, our homes and churches, all educate us and create the context in which our schools operate, supporting them or undermining them as the case may be. A genuine "education society" means something more than a society with good schools. It means a society with a healthy sense of the common good, with social morale and public spirit, and with a vivid memory of its own cultural past. Schools can contribute to that, but they cannot create it out of whole cloth and should not be expected to. Only a further democratic transformation of all our institutions will make possible a genuine "education society. (Robert Bellah, et al., The Good Society)

Education has come a long way since the time of our preindustrial past where, as philosopher John Dewey noted, the practical daily routines of preindustrial life were themselves educative. In contrast, education today functions as a separate and isolated institution. Typically, education takes place inside a brick building in which movement from one subject to the next is marked off by the ringing of a bell in a fixed sequence over the course of the school day. Furthermore, modern education is focused on specialized abstract knowledge set off from wider everyday experience. As Robert Bellah and his associates note in *The Good Society*, the source from which the above quote was taken, advances in science and technology long ago made obsolete the need to gather water for household use, cut firewood for the kettle or stove in which meals were laboriously prepared, or in which water was heated in order to clean bodies, clothes, or dishes. Technological advances also spurred the growth of public provisions serving the home and today provide running water at the turn of a faucet; electric and gas service that makes possible home heating and cooling as well as the use of appliances, lighting, and electronic devices, all at the flip of a switch. Technology has also provided us with sewers and sanitation, along with transportation and communication systems. The irony of all these advances is that they have also given us a false sense of independence and personal autonomy as we go about our daily lives—we become aware of our mutual interdependence and of our greater dependence on institutions only when these systems fail us.

One development in the modern world that seems to serve an educative function is a vast mass media complex that includes radio, television, film, and the Internet. We also have many new means of personal communication that are rooted in these and other media, including mobile phones with Web browsing and texting capability, along with social media such as Facebook. In many ways, these are wonderful and useful technological advances; on the other hand, they raise new dilemmas. Most forms of mass media, for example, have been underwritten (funded) by advertising that is intended to fuel the growth of a vast consumer economy. Moreover, people engage with various types of mass media at increasingly younger ages, and our lives are more thoroughly saturated by marketing and advertising than ever. The fact is that we live in a world in which we are confronted by branded images at virtually every turn. In this world, advertising driven media encourage us to prefer being entertained over being informed, and this diminishes our capacity (let alone our willingness) to develop a society in which all institutional realms are truly educative in a meaningful sense.

Roughly a century ago John Dewey envisioned the challenge for schools was to make the burgeoning industrial society as intelligible to us as the preindustrial world was to its inhabitants. Certainly, the challenges are great, but we should not overlook the enormous privileges we enjoy today because knowledge has been greatly democratized and made accessible for common citizens. As Bellah (quoting Dewey) points out, we only need to go back a few centuries to find "a practical monopoly of learning," or "a high priesthood of learning, which guarded the treasury of truth and which doled it out to the masses under severe restrictions." Today, virtually the opposite is the case, as we are awash in our own modern version of a world of learning. However, this world is generally experienced as bits and fragments of information, and a sea of media images. The overarching reality of our expansive education system is that knowledge and learning have become abstract, specialized, and fragmented. The challenge is to make meaning out the myriad sources of information, and to develop ways to integrate them into some larger interpretive framework, so that we can make sound judgments about the wide array of issues we confront in all aspects of our lives and in society. Here we take up two central institutions impacting the process: education and the mass media.

EDUCATION AS A SOCIAL INSTITUTION

As a core pillar of modern society, the social institution of **education** is a means by which society transmits knowledge and learning to its members. This may take a variety of forms, including practical knowledge that individuals make use of in carrying out productive activity in the economy or which simply aids them in their efforts to carry out basic activities demanded of adults in society. It may take the form of lessons in civics and citizenship, as well as in the transmission of values and norms widely shared throughout society. Once again, as was noted in the introduction to this chapter, education can take place in a variety of contexts. In advanced industrial societies like the United States, education takes place through **schooling**, where students are given instruction on formal subject matter by trained teachers.

In *Society: The Basics*, sociologist John J. Macionis describes some widely accepted functions performed by the system of schooling that serve and support the maintenance of society. Ever since the Industrial Revolution, advances in scientific knowledge and the development of new technologies have accelerated to such an extent that formal schooling with trained teachers is essential for society to *transmit* a rapidly developing *knowledge* base to its citizens. This process also includes changes in our broader cultural understandings about society. In many respects, schooling serves to integrate a diverse population, one that has historically included new immigrants with each succeeding generation, through the transmission and modification of shared *norms and values*. In Chapter 1, we discussed sociologist Robin Williams' delineation of key American values. Two values of great relevance to the realm of education are *equal opportunity* (the chance for all individuals to get ahead in society) and *meritocracy*, which rewards those who work hard and demonstrate their talents.

Critics of schooling in the United States have generally argued the system does not support individual achievement through equal opportunity. It has, on the contrary, had the opposite effect—that is, perpetuating social inequality along with social control. *Standardized testing* and *tracking* (putting students into different types of educational programs within the same school system) are perfect examples of schooling practices that actually reinforce already existing social inequality: Standardized tests generally reflect the knowledge base and understandings of the dominant culture, which often puts minority, working class, and poor students at a disadvantage. This, in turn, often leads the

Formal schooling is an integral element of modern life as societies depend upon the generation and transmission of complex systems of knowledge that are constantly evolving. *(Shutterstock)*

schools to place students with low scores on standardized tests into lower tracks that focus on vocational and technical training rather than college preparatory classes. Such classes may serve their needs and interests, but the practice also serves to cut off avenues to higher levels of academic achievement, and this may ultimately limit their access to economic success. With respect to social control, critics have pointed to the early rise of formal schooling as an accommodation suited to the needs of factory owners, who demanded that the schools first and foremost inculcate values such as obedience, self-discipline, and punctuality. These critics further contend that schools have adopted a bureaucratic organizational model that mirrors that of the factory system.

Schooling: A Historical Background

Today most of us take for granted that young people spend much of their lives in school. This, of course, was not always the case. Nor was the common perception we have that pretty much equates education with schooling. As noted in the beginning of the chapter, this view of schooling places an enormous burden on our schools and does not support the wider notion of education as some-

Up though the nineteenth century, the U.S. was primarily an agrarian society in which life on the farm, in and of itself, was educative, and formal schooling played a less prominent role in the life of the nation. *(Library of Congress)*

thing we need to realize our full potential as a democratic society. The history of schooling follows closely along with the story of the great transformation to modernity discussed in Chapter 2, and with it the shift from a preindustrial to industrial world. And it is in exploring this history that we can determine where and to what extent schooling and education parted company and moved in different directions.

The Rise of Formal Education with the Shift from Preindustrial to Industrial America

One major factor that made possible the historical growth and expansion of America's schools was the nation's growing affluence. Another was industrialization. During our nation's preindustrial past, most people either lived on farms or were engaged in agricultural pursuits of some sort. This dynamic changed greatly with the rise of industrialization in the late nineteenth century, and by 1900 only 40 percent of the working population was engaged in farming. By 1930 that farming population had decreased to about 20; by 1950 it was down to 10 percent. Since 1970, an even smaller percent of the working population has been engaged in agriculture at any given time.

Bellah notes that in 1890 only 7 percent of America's high school age children actually went to high school, and only 1 percent attended college. Over the course of the past century the number of those attending high school and college increased dramatically. By 1918, as Macionis points out, all states had passed mandatory education laws requiring that children attend school until completion of eighth grade or until reaching the age of sixteen. The system of formal education continued to expanded, and by 1950, roughly one-third of the mature adult population were high school graduates and 6 percent had completed college. By the turn of the twenty-first century, those percentages increased to roughly 85 percent for high school graduates and 25 percent for college graduates.

University education also underwent significant changes. Historically, university education was the domain of a very small subset of elites in society. Furthermore, in its classical manifestation the university provided a culturally enriching education focusing on the arts, humanities, and philosophy. It also emphasized character building and virtues such as aesthetic beauty, along with ethical and moral insight. By the late nineteenth century, this classical–cultural model of university education was being overtaken by a formal scientific one. This shift was accompanied by a parallel demise in the older and widely educative forms of learning and knowing, described by John Dewey—education achieved through ordinary every day practices in the home and in the neighborhood, at church, and from doing productive work.

Emblematic of this shift away from a **classical cultural model of knowledge** towards one emphasizing the **rational scientific model** was the rise of the research university in the closing decades of the nineteenth century. New and dynamic institutions geared to this new model emerged on the scene, including Johns Hopkins and Cornell, along with new state universities in Michigan and Wisconsin. Even established institutions such as Harvard and Columbia made the shift toward this new educational paradigm. One driving force for this change was the increased collaboration between science and industry. Bellah notes, for example, that John Dewey joined the University of Chicago with the purpose of advancing his ideals about democracy and education aimed at full participation in society. Dewey was successful in establishing a high degree of interdisciplinary communication and collaboration, along with a strong commitment to the affairs of the wider community. With Dewey's departure, however, the university, like other research universities, continued its drift away from Dewey's holistic vision for education and gave way to increasing specialization. As a result, interest in the wider affairs of the community began to wane and the university came to mirror the wider industrial society—increasingly specialized, fragmented, and bureaucratized.

The Triumph of Today's Research University

The United States has myriad colleges and universities that focus on teaching, as well as numerous and diverse research universities. Arguably one of the finest achievements of this widespread and diverse system of higher education is the fact that many of these institutions, which were once open exclusively to society's wealthy upper class are now accessible to the society at large. This transformation, which began in the early 1950s, shortly after the end of World War II, dramatically changed the face of the "typical" college or university student. Since that time, U.S. colleges and universities have become a vehicle through which individuals from a wide range of social backgrounds work hard, demonstrate their talents, and enter the professional and managerial sectors of the economy by becoming engineers, doctors, lawyers, scientists, accountants, business executives, teachers, and professors. Clearly, this notion of success is a pivotal element of the American dream. However, as Bellah laments, "to focus exclusively on education as a means to advancement in an ever more complex occupational system, itself a function of an ever more complex industrial and postindustrial division of labor, is to leave many other questions unanswered."

The research university came of age with the large corporation, but over much of the past century it was understood that the two had rather different purposes and aims. Over the past several decades, however, those differences have blurred, in part because it has become harder to think about any institution (except perhaps the family) in terms distinct from the economy and the business corporation. Hence, we generally find today that higher education is understood to be a kind of industry, where delivering a product (or menu of offerings) to serve educational consumers (or customers) with an emphasis on productivity and cost effectiveness are the central aims of the operation. The anomaly here lies in the fact that institutions are educative in that they shape students' aims and purposes and understanding of self. But there is a very thin line that separates the educative from the industrial mode: If universities and schools, already organized bureaucratically, immerse themselves exclusively in the language, purposes, and practices of business and accounting, these become the only terms by which students in those schools and universities come to understand themselves, their own goals and aspirations, and their relationship to the wider society.

One particularly interesting aspect of the U.S. educational system is the research university, which (with government support) has played a central institutional role in fueling the technological advancements that made the U.S. economy the envy of the world during the period starting just after World War II. Ironically, a good measure of the scientific-creative advances in science that have served business interests so well, were made possible because our scientists have generally been accorded a significant measure of academic freedom and are therefore somewhat removed from narrow business interests.

Current Debates: Savage Inequalities, Underperforming Schools, and Choice Movements

Our historical account of the rise of schooling and the evolution of the institution of education over the past century or more have focused mostly on the role of the university in society. And while there are concerns today as to whether our universities are providing adequate education and preparation for young adults to thrive in a twenty-first century society, there have been greater concerns over the recent past about that state of our schools at the primary and secondary levels.

One particularly troubling problem in our nation's schools has to do with what scholar Jonathan Kozol refers to as "savage inequalities," in his book of the same name. Kozol's work is very personal. He has spent his career chronicling the vast inequities in the wider American system of primary and secondary education, and his books leave one wondering whether the American value of equal opportunity reads like a hollow and broken slogan in some quarters. For instance, Kozol points out how some of our poorest schools are in the heart of many major U.S. cities such as New York, located in neighborhoods that invariably have the highest levels of poverty and are overwhelmingly populated by minority residents, most typically African Americans and Latinos. The deplorable conditions of some of our schools and the scant opportunities for meaningful educational experiences offered in those schools amount to a national disgrace. Such schools are oftentimes located in makeshift buildings, with leaky roofs and poor lighting. They frequently operate well over capacity, with class sizes oftentimes too large for classrooms to accommodate and for the teachers to manage. In such schools, children regularly deal with inconveniences such as inadequate lunchroom facilities, no gymnasiums, and even no outdoor playgrounds, compounded by dysfunctional heating and cooling systems that mean chilly classrooms in the winter and sweltering heat at the beginning and end of the school year. What is even more discouraging is that Kozol reports that the children in these schools know that the wider society seems to care little about their problems.

In some respects, there have been genuine efforts aimed at improving underperforming schools, and of course, the schools facing the most savage inequalities are invariably underperforming. Furthermore, these efforts seem generally informed by the same constrained business–economic logic that has come to characterize the way in which universities are managed today. One of the most significant efforts in recent years has been the "No Child Left Behind" program created under the administration of former president George W. Bush. This program required regular annual standardized testing of children in reading, math, and science. Schools not demonstrating improvement in their overall test scores were likely to receive some financial aid, but ultimately their low-income students would be allowed to transfer to other schools. Some low-income parents saw this as a golden opportunity to transfer their children into one of a limited number of **charter schools,** public schools that have been given special funding and permission to try innovative approaches and programs. Furthermore, **for-profit schools,** literally schools run by private businesses for the purposes of profit (different from private schools which oftentimes have a unique educational or religious mission) have grown substantially over recent years. In keeping with the business model of education, CEOs (chief executive officers) of these schools argue that they can operate them more efficiently by using an explicit business model to offer an educational product to their customers. One advantage that such schools often have over traditional public schools is that they do not have to take all comers, whereas the historical democratic mission of public education means that the public schools must serve all of our children. Findings on the effectiveness of for-profit schools have been mixed at best, but they have had some success in limited contexts.

Clearly, some of the problems facing our most troubled schools cannot be simply diagnosed and remedied through the evaluation and narrow improvement in test scores. Schools are part of a wider institutional context in society, one that was once understood to be broadly educative. However, as we have narrowed the focus of education to schooling, our understanding of the wider democratic challenges and the potential solutions to problems in education has also become extremely narrow.

We now turn to another institutional context that has significant implications for the wider institutional context of education in society—that of the mass media, which we earlier noted served both an educative function and increasingly poses a challenge. The purpose of this brief section on the mass media is to raise awareness about the sources of mass media content and images, and the driving or motivating interests behind them. We will also consider some of the possibilities and implications of contemporary forms of media that are overtaking television's central role in our lives.

THE INSTITUTION OF THE MASS MEDIA

Mass media is a means for delivering impersonal communications to a vast audience. As sociologist John Macionis notes, mass media emerged from developments in communications technology that had the capacity to spread information on a mass scale. Such media include newspapers, radio, television, film, and the Internet. Many sociologists treat the mass media, along with the family, the peer group, and the school, as major *agents of socialization.* That is they are central to the process by which people develop their human potential and learn about their culture.

Around the 1950s, television became the dominant medium in U.S. society. Today, almost 100 percent of U.S. households have one or more televisions, with over 80 percent having cable or satellite service. The average household has a television on for more than eight hours a day, and Americans on average spend half their free time watching television (although young people are increasingly consuming other media, such as video games, and are spending time on the computer, often cruising the Internet).

Corporations, Media Empires, and the Marketing Imperative

Today's mass media environment is dominated by a few global media corporations, each of which has holdings in virtually every media industry imaginable, ranging from newspapers to television and radio, book publishing, and the Internet. The fundamental aim of these corporations is profitability, and so marketing and advertising considerations are central to virtually all aspects of their programming decisions. Although it can be justifiably argued that the current global media environment has led to enormous increases in consumer choice, the creative shaping of those choices is driven almost exclusively by one overarching commercial logic. This logic pretty much dictates that everything produced by the mass media be dedicated to selling something. This situation, viewed in conjunction with the demise of a viable countervailing power (discussed in Chapter 4), raises serious concerns about the wider educative and democratic functions of the mass media today.

The corporate controlled mass media has exacerbated the tension between editorial, creative, and even democratic values and commercial values in several ways. One of these involves the traditional function of mass media outlets as a public service provider—specifically as a reliable source of news, an essential element of democratic society. Several decades ago, the three major networks, ABC, NBC, and CBS, dominated the television news landscape. Their news divisions included expensive operations that were not necessarily expected to be profitable, but their journalistic function was valued and supported as a part of the cost and social responsibility associated with running a major network. In tandem with this, Americans supported a myriad of local and national newspapers. Both television and print news outlets dedicated substantial resources to reports from the field, which typically required what has been known as shoe-leather reporting.

Over time, major media outlets in both print and television journalism were consolidated, with larger media corporations typically buying up smaller ones and then streamlining their operations. One result of this consolidation was a redefinition of purpose—new and larger corporate owners quickly began to see commercial values as paramount for their operation and survival. Today, increased competition and a more exclusive focus on profits has meant that news organizations have a more difficult time producing original, localized, investigative stories utilizing experienced reporters. Furthermore, traditional news outlets must now compete for younger audiences that tend to get their news online. One new promising development has been the rise of blogs devoted to news and politics on the Web, but these outlets also suffer from limited resources for staff and reporters.

Another way in which the corporate dominated mass media has extended commercial values is by targeting children and teen markets, with an especially strong explosion of marketing and advertising directed at young children. Before cable television, the major networks tended to provide children's programming only once or twice a week, broadcasting Saturday morning cartoons or the occasional weekday afternoon child-friendly programming. It wasn't until cable television became widely available in the 1970s and 1980s that there were separate cable channels dedicated exclusively to children. Today, there are many such channels, and their programming for children is broadcast 24/7. Accompanying this new focus on children has been an intensification of advertising and marketing efforts directed specifically at children. Many media companies employ a synergistic marketing method, building their advertising efforts around something familiar and entertaining, like, for instance, a Disney movie. This approach encourages children to want dolls and action figures based on the main characters of a favorite film, or to want fast-food meals that are themed to the movie and include little prizes. Furthermore, many children's programs are themselves "themed." They are based on movies and their merchandise or on popular toys and action figures. This goes on to such an extent that it has become difficult to tell the difference between the entertainment and the merchandising. Programming for older children follows suit. Many tween idols in music and film are the creation of corporate marketing campaigns that tie in music, videos, movies, and television shows all in one multifaceted package.

If you think that teenagers are too independent minded and market and media savvy to fall for the advertising messages of large corporations and their ploys, think again. One of the most pervasive and concerted campaigns on the part of media corporations over the past two decades has been to capture and thoroughly permeate the teen and young adult market. And it is a very successful campaign indeed. The methods used by media companies to pull this off is well captured by the PBS documentary series, *Frontline*, and particularly a 2001 special entitled "The Merchants of Cool." In this special, media experts Mark Crispin Miller, author of *Boxed In: The Culture of TV*, and Robert McChesney, author of *Rich Media, Poor Democracy*, describe these very successful media/advertising tactics. Miller emphasizes that "Kids grow up in a universe that is utterly suffused with commercial propaganda. And by that I mean, not only the ads per se, but the shows that sell the ads. What this system does is it closely studies the young, keeps them under very tight surveillance to figure out what will push their buttons. Then it takes that and blares it back at them relentlessly and everywhere."

Our 21st-Century Digital World

Another more recent (2010) installment of *Frontline*, entitled "Digital Nation," notes how "within a single generation, digital media and the World Wide Web have transformed virtually every aspect of modern culture, from the way we learn and work to the ways in which we socialize and even conduct war." If you have a hard time imagining a world outside of one rich in the use of digital media (texting, Web browsing, iTunes, etc.) you are more than likely a *digital native*, someone who came of age with a host of digital media and feels very comfortable being immersed in it and navigating though it. By contrast, a *digital immigrant* is someone who came of age without being immersed in digital media and generally never feels quite as comfortable or at home with it as a native does. This difference parallels the difference between native speakers of a language and those who came to learn that language later in life.

Our new world of digital media (which many digital natives view as "the world,") presents a host of new possibilities for organizing and understanding social life and the social self, and these possibilities have profound implications for culture and society. One of the outgrowths of contemporary digital media is a world that provides full-time access to information and to other people. You can make friends or communicate with relatives anywhere around the world at a moment's notice. You can maintain connections with your parents or your friends instantly, in real time, any time, and anywhere you might be (for example, while you are reading this book, even if you are by yourself, in the library).

Furthermore, it has been argued that digital media have the potential to enhance democratic processes and practices. And, in truth, it provides us with

Corporate advertising and marketing specialists have ventured into just about every nook and cranny of our lives in their efforts to shape their messages and market their products. This process, depicted roughly a decade ago in the PBS Frontline documentary "The Merchants of Cool," has only intensified with the growth of the online world and interactive social media, as data-mining companies have the ability to troll endless sources of user activity and then utilize that data to serve marketing and advertising interests. *(Shutterstock)*

many options and opportunities to explore this potential. We can, for example, access a rich and diverse blogosphere where we can seek out alternative inter pretations and analysis to the mainstream media. More dramatically, digital media have been associated with facilitating democratic social movements around the world, most recently in the Middle East, as authoritarian government regimes find it increasingly difficult to control information and news that can now be transmitted via satellite television, through Facebook or Twitter, or by text messaging. Those authoritarian governments must now contend with diverse interpretations and criticisms of their policies, which can be seen, read, and heard all over the world.

On the other hand, the increased number of media outlets and voices on the Internet add to the fragmentation of knowledge, and perhaps too much of it. Some would argue that we have become overwhelmed by a sea of information and have not yet found a way of ordering it in a meaningful and coherent manner. In addition, those of us who are digital natives are far more likely to prefer a life of multitasking, which means maintaining connections and involvement

Consider the deeper social implications of the new electronic media. We now have the potential to connect with distant others anytime, anywhere, but we also run the risk of disconnecting from those closest to us. *(Shutterstock)*

with multiple forms of digital media while doing something else, whether that something else be studying, driving a car, attending a class, or partaking in a family dinner at home. This mode of operating creates fragmented learning and perhaps a fragmented way of life. Interestingly, "Digital Nation" points to studies by psychologists that indicate we are not nearly as effective at multitasking as we believe ourselves to be.

We are just beginning to understand how our digital world is reshaping human interaction and human relationships. We have already discussed the enormous potential to connect with distant others or keep in touch with friends and family in real time. Furthermore, the digital world has made it possible for some to find greater intimacy and personal fulfillment by connecting to physically distant others whom they may or may not one day meet in person. Sometimes this is achieved through shared interests online, or even through partaking in fantasy worlds, such as "World of Warcraft" or "Second Life." But sociologist Sherry Turkle, who has been studying the online world for decades now, raises concerns about how our immersion in and use of myriad digital technologies is changing the texture of our interactions, the meaning of our close relationships, and our ability to think with intellectual depth and clarity. These changes all seem to be evolving in a manner directed towards shortened, clipped, fleeting, and superficial communication, much like that seen in a text message.

Digital technology can make us feel empowered and can provide a heretofore impossible degree of personal freedom. But we must also be aware that digital technologies are increasingly controlled by big corporations engaged in life or death struggles to increase profitability and expand market share. Core consumer values, along with marketing and advertising activities, are their main concern. And so, the more we participate in various forms of digital media, the more likely we can assume that our Web searches, Facebook postings, book purchases, music downloads, and blog visits, will be recorded, analyzed and marketed by data-mining companies and sold to the highest bidder. Over time, we may lose a sense of personal space or privacy, because those corporations that run and manage the digital universe can be counted on to shape it in ways that will maximize profitability but not necessarily enhance democracy.

CONCLUSIONS: OUR EDUCATION/KNOWLEDGE SOCIETY

Right from the outset of this chapter, you have been encouraged to consider the educative functions of our wider social institutions. We also explored how with the rise of industrialization and modern life, the fading of our preindustrial past meant the loss of many aspects of daily institutional life that were truly and practically educative. Over the course of the past century education has increasingly come to mean schooling. Furthermore, the growing centrality of the scientific model of education, along with increased specialization due to the explosive growth in fields of knowledge, combined with bureaucratic methods of administering schools, colleges, and universities, has meant an increasing fragmentation and abstraction of the learning process. This condition of advanced modern society also co-exists with the growth and increasing dominance of mass media, which has served an educative function while raising new questions and challenges over the past century. The rise of large scale media empires has transformed many forms of media, especially television news and programming, into service of marketing and advertising imperatives aimed at generating profits. New digital media have offered some hope for a new more fulfilling, intensively social, information rich, if not accelerated mode of living.

And yet, we must ultimately confront how this educative media is also increasingly being controlled by large corporations that are locked in titanic and global struggles to claim precious market share and advertising revenues that fuel their profitability. In the end, our greatest challenge is to continuously strive to maintain and reinvigorate the democratic promise, which depends upon an informed citizenry.

Further Reading

Bellah. Robert N., Richard Madsen, William M. Sullivan, Ann Swidler, and Steven M. Tipton. *The Good Society.* New York: Alfred A. Knopf, 1991.

Kozol, Jonathan. *Savage Inequalities: Children in America's Schools.* New York: Harper Collins, 1991.

_____. *The Shame of the Nation: The Restoration of Apartheid Schooling in America.* New York: Random House, 2005.

Macionis, John J. *Society: The Basics.* 10th ed. Upper Saddle River, N.J.: Prentice Hall, 2009.

McChesney, Robert W. *Rich Media, Poor Democracy: Communication Politics in Dubious Times.* New York: The New Press, 2000.

Miller, Mark Crispin. *Boxed In: The Culture of TV.* Chicago: Northwestern University Press, 1988.

Turkle, Sherry. *Life on Screen: Identity in the Age of the Internet.* New York: Touchstone, 1995.

_____. *Alone Together: Why We Expect More from Technology and Less from Each Other,* New York: Basic Books, 2011.

CHAPTER 7

CONCLUSIONS

In this volume we have come to see how social structure, as a basic building block of society, is expressed through institutions and organizations in the modern world. Hopefully, this has given you an appreciation of how the basic nature of social institutions today must be understood—first though the great transformation to modernity and then through the associated growth of rationalized, complex, and typically bureaucratic organizations. Today, that same transformation can also be understood as the McDonaldization of society. In this book, we have also laid bare the foundation upon which social institutions, the fundamentally structured arenas of social life, have been cast for our contemporary world. Understanding this foundation is a vital component for understanding the promises and possibilities of the future.

This book has also delved into the characteristic qualities of modern life that have led to social fragmentation and a rationalization of society. But the ability to confront the modern world with an understanding of its historical institutional foundations will help to enable us to become responsible and informed citizens who have the ability to confront a promising yet perilous future.

Institutions are certainly structured, and in today's world, that structure oftentimes takes on the form of a complex organization, run more or less along bureaucratic lines. However, institutions are not stagnant. Instead, they change and evolve over time. Sometimes they evolve to solve new problems or to support new opportunities, or some combination of both. At other times we seem to be stuck with older notions about the nature of a given institution that informally teaches us about who we are, what we should desire, and how the institution in question can help fulfill that desire. For instance, many of us still harbor romantic notions about a long gone yeoman democracy of small independent farmers or entrepreneurs. But we hold onto this very alluring image of our world at the cost of not realistically confronting the current world, which is characterized by celebrated entrepreneurs who have generated businesses that have come to dominate national, even international markets, spanning the globe. In fact, some of these celebrated entrepreneurs have become part of a new global elite, whose interests, unfortunately, are seldom tied to those of their fellow citizens. And yet, with the growing prominence of the corporate mass media, the lives and aspirations of this elite are perpetuated as idealized images for all to consume. In the process, the wider educative function of the mass media has been eclipsed by a focus on entertainment and advertising, making meaningful and wider ranging deliberation about the realm of politics and government well nigh impossible. Education, which at the tertiary (university) level in the United States is still the envy of the world, also faces many challenges, especially with respect to serving the needs of our most vulnerable and marginalized citizens. And perhaps, what is most needed to support the education of those experiencing savage inequalities today, is to find ways of providing stable, secure, employment for their parents and their communities.

In the end, our efforts to understand contemporary social structures, the organizational and institutional foundations upon which our social world rests, and their potential contribution toward meeting the needs of society, will require taking what we have learned from this volume, and expanding beyond it. In this volume, our understanding of social structure has implicitly been approached from a national, or nation-state, context. As readers grow and continue to advance their understanding of social structure, institutions, and organizations, the next challenge will be to extend these concepts to a global or international context.

GLOSSARY

achieved status   A social position assumed by a person through talent or effort.

actor   A unique and complex individual who is part of a social population or society.

affectivity or affective neutrality   A pair of pattern variables which determine how behavior is oriented, depending on whether or not emotional gratification can be expected from a relationship.

ascribed status   A social position assigned to a person either at birth or later in life over which that person has little control.

ascription or achievement   A pair of pattern variables that orient behavior on the basis of ascribed or achieved characteristics.

authoritarianism   A system of government that denies people formal rights.

authority   Political power that is recognized and accepted as legitimate by those over whom it is exercised.

beliefs   Statements held by a group to be true.

bourgeoisie   Members of an economic class consisting of small shopkeepers, merchants, and factory owners, all of whom earn profits instead of wages.

bureaucracy   An organizational model based upon hierarchy, rules and regulations, and extensive specialization, aimed at achieving efficiency.

calculability   A principle of McDonaldization emphasizing quantifiable aspects of some product or service over the vaguer and more ambiguous principle of quality.

capitalism   An economic system in which labor, goods, and services are exchanged between buyers and sellers in a marketplace, and which depends upon private ownership of property.

charter schools   Public schools that have been given special allowances to try innovative approaches and programs.

churches   Religious organizations that are integrated into the wider society.

classical cultural model of knowledge-education   An approach to university education with a strong emphasis upon the arts, humanities, and philosophy, a concern with character building, and an emphasis upon virtues such as aesthetic beauty coupled with the development of ethical and moral insight.

coercive organization   An organization that must rely upon force or coercion to motivate, direct, and control the actions of its members.

collectivity or self   A pair of pattern variables that orient behavior toward individual or collective goals or ends.

competition   A form of social interaction where the parties involved struggle to achieve some goal or reward not available to all, but do so within a clearly defined set of rules or norms.

conflict   A form of interaction in which the ends or goals of the interacting parties are in opposition, and in which each may utilize force, violence, or other coercive means.

constitutional monarchy   A system of government with a monarch who serves as the head of state but whose powers are delimited by a constitution.

control   A principle of McDonaldization that focuses on the use of organizational practices, along with the implementation of new technologies, in order to ensure the predictable and efficient delivery of services.

cooperation   A form of social interaction where the parties involved share the same mutually beneficial goal.

cottage work   Small-scale home-based production common during preindustrial times.

culture   The beliefs, values, norms, symbols, language, material objects, and technology that define the life of a group.

democracy   A political system that grants power to the people as a whole. Core principles that inform democracy are individual freedom and equality, as well as a voice for all people in directing the nation's affairs.

diffuseness or specificity   A pair of pattern variables that orient behavior on the basis of diffuse and highly variable demands or demands that are narrowly defined and specified.

economy   The social institution in which the production, distribution, and consumption of goods and services are organized.

education   The social institution through which society transmits knowledge and learning to its members.

efficiency   A principle of McDonaldization concerned with the creation of organizational systems and practices aimed at achieving narrowly defined goals in the most cost-effective manner.

family   A social institution in which emotional, physical, and/or economic support is provided to members, binding them into a primary group, and socializing them for participation in the wider society.

folkways   Practices and customs that guide the everyday activities of a group.

for-profit schools   Schools run by private businesses for profit.

formal organizations   Large secondary groups that are organized around a specific goal or purpose.

government   The organized means through which politics are carried out and administered.

hierarchy of authority   An element of bureaucracy in which there exists a clear chain of command that defines the levels of decision-making responsibility present throughout an organization.

impersonality   An element of bureaucracy requiring that bureaucrats function without hatred, passion, affection, or enthusiasm in carrying out their duties to an organization. The same element dictates that clients be treated as cases and given neither special nor adverse treatment.

incest taboo   A norm that forbids sexual relations and/or marriage between certain relatives.

industrialization   A historical process dating back to the Industrial Revolution in which a new type of dynamic and productive economic system transformed virtually every aspect of society.

institutions   Major arenas of social life that have distinctive goals, ends, or purposes, and which consist of related clusters of normative expectations and distinctive sets of interrelated statuses.

Keynesianism   An economic theory named after famous British economist John Maynard Keynes, emphasizing the need for an active government role in directing and intervening into the affairs of the capitalist economy.

kinship   A condition in which people are related to one another based upon common ancestry, marriage, or adoption.

laissez-faire   A French term which means to leave or let alone and reflects a form of capitalism in which government plays a minimal role in the affairs of the economy.

marriage   A legal consensual relationship, usually involving some combination of economic cooperation, sexual activity, and childbearing.

mass media   A vehicle for delivering impersonal communications to a vast audience.

master status   A social position having special and powerful significance for virtually every aspect of an individual's life.

McDonaldization   A term coined by George Ritzer, which refers to how the principles of the fast food restaurant are coming to dominate virtually all sectors of society.

means-end social action   A social action that involves viewing other people, as well as all aspects of the material world, as a means to achieving one's rationally calculated ends or goals in the most efficient manner possible.

monarchy   A system of government in which a single individual or family holds absolute power to rule.

mores   Norms having great moral significance for a group.

negative sanctions   Penalties exacted for violating social norms.

normative organization   An organization primarily dedicated to a mission or goals that are deemed as good, admirable, and morally worthwhile by its members.

norms   Rules for behavior; the dos and don'ts of everyday life.

oligarchy   A system of government in which a small group or class rules.

particularism or universalism   A pair of pattern variables that guide behavior by particular, unique, or personal qualities of relationships or on the basis of a universal set of standards or criteria.

pattern variables   A schema developed by Talcott Parsons reflecting decisions that individuals must make in orienting their behavior in various social situations before taking some course of action.

political economy   A term embraced by economists up through the late nineteenth century to emphasize that economy is part of the larger fabric of social life and is interrelated with other institutional domains, especially politics and government.

politics   A social institution that defines values, sets priorities, and establishes goals all with the aim of mobilizing resources for achieving the collective ends or purposes of a society.

positive sanctions   Rewards given for observing social norms.

predictability   A principle of McDonaldization that emphasizes uniformity in the production and delivery of services.

primary groups   Small cooperative groups characterized by intimate, face-to-face, association.

primary sector   An area of economic activity that includes agriculture, along with raw material and resource extraction from the natural environment.

profane   The ordinary and commonplace elements of the everyday social world.

Protestant ethic   Max Weber's term for a highly disciplined and rationalized work ethic that is informed by a religious belief system.

rational-legal authority   A form of political authority in which elected officials owe their obedience to what is commonly referred to as the rule of law.

rational life orientation   An approach to living that is guided by principles of rational calculation, efficiency, and control.

rational scientific model of education   An approach to university education that accompanied the rise of the research university; a growing shift in emphasis toward abstract scientific knowledge and away from arts and humanities.

rationalization of society   A process accompanying industrialization in which social life has become ever more impersonal and society is increasingly organized around principles of rational calculation, efficiency, and control.

red tape   A problem associated with bureaucracy, usually created by an endless accumulation of rules and regulations that can lead both the organization's personnel and its clients to become confused, frustrated, and demoralized.

religion   Defined by sociologist Emile Durkheim as a unified system of beliefs and practices relative to sacred things.

representative democracy   A form of democracy in which citizens elect representatives to independent ruling bodies. These representatives are charged with carrying out the will of the people.

rites   Rituals marking symbolic transitions between phases in social life.

rituals   Formal ceremonial behavior involving the sacred.

role(s)   Behaviors and expectations associated with a given status.

role distance   The process of detaching oneself from a role even as one engages in it, signaling to oneself and others that the role is in no way aligned with one's identity.

role embracement   Enacting a role in such a way that it reflects, verifies, and defines an important aspect of one' identity.

rule of law   A doctrine wherein formally enacted legal rules and principles define the nature and degree of decision-making authority granted to governing officials.

rules and regulations   An element of bureaucracy through which an organization explicitly defines all aspects of its operation and processes clients and paperwork (the files) in a clear and consistent manner.

sacred   A social domain transcending everyday life and containing elements that are set apart and inspire awe and reverence.

sanctions   Rewards or penalties given or exacted for affirming or violating social norms.

schooling   A system in which professionally trained teachers provide formal instruction to students.

scientific management   A managerial approach developed by F.W. Taylor in which the activities involved in any task are broken down into their simplest elements and reconfigured through careful experimental observation into the most efficient sequence possible.

second wave in the great Industrial Revolution   An era that involved new systems of organizational control aimed at adapting the workforce to meet the demanding pace and enormous capacity of machinery in the factory.

secondary groups   Large and impersonal collectives organized around specific goals or purposes.

secondary sector   An area of economic activity focused on manufacturing in which raw materials are transformed into finished goods.

secularization   A modern-day process through which religion and the scared play an ever-diminishing role in other major institutions and in the lives of individuals.

social stratification   Systems by which societies rank categories of people in a hierarchy.

social structure   Stable and recurring patterns of social behavior.

socialism   A political–economic system in which property and the means to carry out productive activity are collectively owned, and which typically involves centralized government planning.

specialization   An element of bureaucracy involving the creation of a complex division of labor wherein specialized departments and staff take on specialized roles within an organization.

status   A recognized social position occupied by an individual.

status set   All the statuses held by an individual at any given time.

technical–professional experts   Staff that are recruited by a bureaucracy and then trained and evaluated over time on the basis of formal technical criteria in their defined area of expertise.

tertiary sector   An area of economic activity that involves the provision of services as opposed to the production of goods or resource extraction.

totalitarianism   A system of government that denies people formal rights while also extensively controlling their lives.

traditional authority   A form of political authority that is conferred based upon custom and practice.

traditional social action   A type of social action in which behaviors and interactions are defined by habit or custom.

urbanization   The process by which an increasing number of people reside in cities rather than rural areas; most often associated with industrialization.

utilitarian organization   An organization primarily dedicated to profit making.

value rational social action   A type of social action in which some ethical, moral, or religious principle is consciously embraced for its own sake irrespective of whether it enables the achievement of one's narrowly defined ends or goals.

values   Things reflecting group consensus about what is good and desirable in life and that represent the ends or goals of behavior.

BIBLIOGRAPHY

Bellah, Robert N., Richard Madsen, William M. Sullivan, Ann Swidler, and Steven M. Tipton. *The Good Society*. New York: Alfred A. Knopf, 1991.

Berger, Peter L. *The Sacred Canopy: Elements of a Sociological Theory of Religion*. Garden City, N.Y.: Doubleday, 1967.

Bratton, John, David Denham, and Linda Deutschmann. *Capitalism and Classical Sociological Theory*. Toronto: University of Toronto Press, 2009.

Cassidy, John. *How Markets Fail: The Logic of Economic Calamities*. New York: Farrar, Straus, and Giroux, 2009.

Cherlin, Andrew J. "The Deinstitutionalization of American Marriage." *Journal of Marriage and the Family* 66 (2004): 848–861.

_____. *Public and Private Families: An Introduction*. 5th ed. Boston: McGraw-Hill, 2008.

Cooley, Charles H. *Human Nature and the Social Order*. New York: Scribner's, 1922.

Dobriner, William M. *Social Structures and Systems: A Sociological Overview*. Pacific Palisades, Calif.: Goodyear Publishing Company, 1969.

Durkheim, Emile. *The Elementary Forms of Religious Life*. New York: Free Press, [1915] 1965.

Ferguson, Susan J. *Shifting the Center: Understanding Contemporary Families*. 3rd ed. Boston: McGraw Hill, 2007.

Freeland, Chrystia. "The Rise of the New Global Elite." *The Atlantic*. January/February, 2011.

Friedman, Milton. *Capitalism and Freedom*. Chicago: University of Chicago Press, 1962.

Galbraith, John K. *The Essential Galbraith*. Boston: Mariner Books, 2001.

Gibbs, Nancy. "What Women Want Now." *Time*. October 14, 2009.

Giddens, Anthony. *Runaway World*. New York: Routledge, 2000.

Graham, Laurie. *On the Line at Subaru-Isuzu: The Japanese Model and the American Worker*. Ithaca, N.Y.: Cornell University Press, 1995.

Hacker, Jacob S. *The Great Risk Shift: The Assault on American Jobs, Families, Health Care and Retirement And How You Can Fight Back*. Oxford: Oxford University Press, 2006.

Hochschild, Arlie R. *The Second Shift*. New York: Avon, 1989.

Johnson, Simon. "The Quiet Coup." *The Atlantic*. May, 2009.

Kivisto, Peter. *Key Ideas in Sociology*. 2nd ed. Thousand Oaks, Calif.: Pine Forge, 2004.

Kozol, Jonathan. *Savage Inequalities: Children in America's Schools*. New York: Harper Collins, 1991.

Kroc, Ray A. *Grinding it Out: The Making of McDonald's*. Chicago: Contemporary Books, 1977.

Leidner, Robin. *Fast Food, Fast Talk*. Berkeley: University of California Press, 1993.

Macionis, John J. *Society: The Basics*. 10th ed. Upper Saddle River, N.J.: Prentice Hall, 2009.

McChesney, Robert W. *Rich Media, Poor Democracy: Communication Politics in Dubious Times*. New York: The New Press, 2000.

Miller, Mark Crispin. *Boxed In: The Culture of TV*. Chicago: Northwestern University Press, 1988.

Parsons, Talcott. *Toward a General Theory of Action*. Edward A. Shils and T. Parsons (Eds.). Cambridge, Mass.: Harvard University Press, 1951.

Ritzer, George. *The McDonaldization of Society*. Thousand Oaks, Calif.: Pine Forge/Sage, 1993.

_____. *Enchanting a Disenchanted World: Revolutionizing the Means of Consumption*. Thousand Oaks, Calif.: Pine Forge/Sage, 2005.

Schlosser, Eric. *Fast Food Nation: The Dark Side of the All American Meal*. New York: Harper Perennial, 2002.

Turkle, Sherry. *Life on Screen: Identity in the Age of the Internet*. New York: Touchstone, 1995.

_____. *Alone Together: Why We Expect More from Technology and Less from Each Other,* New York: Basic Books, 2011.

Uchitelle, Louis. *The Disposable American.* New York: Alfred A. Knopf, 2006.

Warren, Elizabeth, and Amelia Warren Tyagi. *The Two-Income Trap: Why Middle-Class Mothers and Fathers Are Going Broke.* New York: Basic Books, 2003.

Weber, Max. *The Protestant Ethic and the Spirit of Capitalism.* London: Harper Collins Academic, [1904-1905] 1930.

Womack, James P., Daniel T. Jones, and Daniel Roos. *The Machine that Changed the World.* New York: Rawson Associates, 1990.

INDEX

Index note: Page numbers followed by *g* indicate glossary entries.